SHALL
NEVER
PERISH

Other Books by J. F. Strombeck

DISCIPLINED BY GRACE

FIRST THE RAPTURE

GRACE AND TRUTH

SHALL NEVER PERISH

SO GREAT SALVATION

J. F. Strombeck

SHALL NEVER PERISH

Eternal Security Examined

KREGEL PUBLICATIONS
Grand Rapids, Michigan 49501

Shall Never Perish, by J. F. Strombeck. © 1991 by Kregel Publications, a division of Kregel, Inc., P.O. Box 2607, Grand Rapids, MI 49501. All rights reserved.

Cover Design: Don Ellens

Library of Congress Cataloging-in-Publication Data

Strombeck, J. F. (John Frederick), 1881-1959.
  Shall never perish / by J. F. Strombeck.
      p.   cm.
  Reprint. Originally published: Philadelphia: American Bible Conference Association, c. 1936.

  1. Assurance (Theology) 2. Grace (Theology) 3. Perseverance (Theology) 4. Arminianism—Controversial literature.   I. Title.

| BT811.S76 | 1991 | 234—dc20 | 90-20699 |
| | | | CIP |

ISBN 0-8254-3779-2 (paperback)

1 2 3 4 5 Printing/Year 95 94 93 92 91

Printed in the United States of America

Contents

Part Three
Eternal Security and Godly Living

Part Four
Arguments Against Eternal Security Answered

Part Five
Evils of Arminianism

Conclusion

Foreword

When I was a very young believer, someone introduced me to the books written by J.F. Strombeck, and I bless the day it happened. *Shall Never Perish* settled for me the matter of my security in Christ, and *Grace and Truth* helped me understand the true relationship between law and grace. *Disciplined by Grace* balanced these doctrines for me and delivered me from the extremes some people go to when they first discover grace and assurance. I owe a debt of gratitude to Mr. Strombeck, and I gladly acknowledge it.

John Frederick Strombeck was born in Moline, Illinois, on December 16, 1881, into a pioneer Swedish family. Converted to Christ early in life, J.F. always sought God's leading in his decisions, both personal and business.

He started his own freight auditing business, which he managed for about ten years. When he was 25, he returned to school, first at Northwestern Academy, and then Northwestern University, from which he graduated Phi Beta Kappa in 1911. After his graduation, the Strombeck-Becker Manufacturing Company was born, specializing in various wood products. That same year he married.

J.F.'s first love was ministry in the church and with various Christian organizations that he supported. He served as a director or advisor to the Belgian Gospel Mission, Dallas

Theological Seminary, Moody Bible Institute, Young Life, Inter-Varsity, and many others. While a member of the Evangelical Free Church, he was often invited to minister in the Word in various conferences, and he wrote many articles for Christian publications. The burden of foreign missions lay heavy on his heart, and he was a generous supporter of missionaries and schools that trained missionaries.

You will discover as you read each of his books that J.F. Strombeck, though a layman, had a thorough grasp of Bible doctrine and was able to apply it practically. He did not write books in order to impress, but to express what God taught him, so that you might enjoy the full blessings of salvation in Christ. I suggest that you keep your Bible close at hand as you read Strombeck's books, because he uses the Word from beginning to end!

Though J.F. Strombeck died on May 9, 1959, the investments he made in many evangelical ministries continue to produce spiritual dividends, and his Christ-centered books continue to challenge and instruct serious students of the Word. I rejoice that Kregel Publications is making these helpful volumes available to a new generation of believers.

WARREN W. WIERSBE

SHALL
NEVER
PERISH

1

". . . Shall Never Perish"

M Y SHEEP hear My voice, and I know them, and they follow Me: and I give unto them eternal life; and they shall never perish, and no one shall snatch them out of My hand. My Father, Who hath given them unto Me, is greater than all; and no one is able to snatch them out of the Father's hand" (John 10:27-29 R. V.).

For the believer in the Lord Jesus Christ, no passage in the Bible has more assurance in it than has this one. In it is found an unconditional statement by our Lord that those who are His are His for all eternity, because they are in His hand, under His care, and are in the Father's hand, under His care. The strength of the Father is that which guarantees this condition of safety.

There are those who are not willing to accept this simple and clear statement without modifying it. Thereby they do not only lose the assurance that might come to themselves; but they rob others of that assurance which is so greatly needed by every one of God's children.

God makes two kinds of promises to His children: conditional and unconditional. But He always makes it clear whether or not they are conditional or unconditional. When conditional, He uses the word "if" or its equivalent; but when His statement is unconditional, He leaves out the "if." This is therefore an unconditional statement.

But there are many who, claiming to accept the Bible as being God inspired, nevertheless insist that this is a conditional statement, and that "if" the sheep follow they shall never perish. By what right do they add the word "if"? As it is neither stated nor implied by the context, it is clearly a case of tampering with God's Word, and changing its meaning.

Five separate statements are made concerning "My sheep": (1) Hear My voice, (2) I know them, (3) they follow Me, (4) I give them eternal life and (5) they shall never perish. These are five distinct things said about those who are His sheep. Not one is conditional upon any other.

By adding the word "if" to the third statement, the fourth as well as the fifth must become conditional upon it. Thus not only the question of perishing, but also that of receiving eternal life would be conditional upon following the Lord. Then, to make the words "follow Me" mean the living of a life as the Lord Jesus lived His (as some assert), makes this mean that the one who lives as He lived will *thereby* receive eternal life and shall never perish. This is nothing less than modernism grown to full fruitage. It is salvation by works. Thus this addition of the word "if" denies salvation by grace through faith; it is a denial of the grace of God. It is dangerous to tamper with God's Word!

As though this light handling of God's eternal verities were not enough, it is further being preached and taught that while no one can snatch one of Christ's own out of His hand and out of the Father's hand, it is possible for one to jump out of his own volition. By what scriptural authority is that statement made? Does the wording of the passage permit such a statement? Only two conditions could make it possible for a sheep to jump out of his own accord: (1) that he be given the freedom to do so, or (2) that he have the power to do so against the purpose of God. Are either of these possible?

The sheep belong to Christ; they are "My sheep." They are His because He, the Good Shepherd, gave His life for them. He purchased them with His own blood. And they have been given unto Him by the Father. Ownership means lordship. That which is owned has no right of will contrary to the will of the owner. It has liberty to go, only within the limits granted by the owner. It is perfectly clear then, that the Good Shepherd does not grant to any sheep that has cost Him so much to place in His own hand for safety, the privilege of jumping out of it.

God's hand is not an open hand. It is a hand that holds. When a father or a mother holds the hand of a small child to lead him safely through some place of real danger, that father or mother will not let that little hand go, even though the child might try to pull away.

No, God does not grant the sheep the liberty to jump out of His hand. It would disgrace a human shepherd of sheep to say that he allowed his sheep to stray away from him. How much more does it not disgrace the Good Shepherd to say that He allows His sheep to go away from Him?

The only question left then is, has the sheep the power to leap out of God's hand contrary to His will and purpose? To admit this, would be to contradict Jesus' words: "My Father . . . is greater than all." The "all" necessarily includes the sheep. It also would contradict His words, "they shall never perish," for if they did jump out they must perish.

What a perversion of God's Word it is to add the little word "if" and to limit God by saying that a sheep can jump out of God's hand!

It denies salvation by grace through faith; it denies the fact of a believer's eternal life; it makes the will of man stronger than the will of God; it discounts the keeping power of God, and it robs the believer of his assurance. And yet men, who are called to be ambassadors of God, to be stewards of the manifold grace of God, often very earnestly and zealously, but mistakenly, do that very thing.

Jesus made another statement concerning Himself and His sheep. He said, "The Good Shepherd giveth His life for the sheep" (John 10:11). This statement and the one, "My sheep shall never perish," are inter-dependent upon each other. They are to each other as cause and effect. The one cannot be touched without touching the other. *To deny the effect—the absolute safety of the sheep—is to question the efficacy of the cause—the death of the Good Shepherd.*

When Jesus says, "My sheep shall never perish," it is unconditional and final. It is to be accepted in simple faith and made the subject of rejoicing and thanksgiving.

2

Why This Discussion?

THE TRUTH that "My sheep . . . shall never perish," and that "no one is able to snatch them out of the Father's hand," is the substance of the doctrine of eternal security of the believer. Some object to a discussion of this doctrine on the ground that it engenders controversy and is not essential to salvation. It is true that as far as those who have been saved are concerned, they are still saved whether they understand this doctrine or not; but it has been the experience of multitudes that they have not *known* whether or not they are saved until they have come to understand this precious truth. In fact, without spiritual understanding of this doctrine it is impossible for any one to be assured of eternal glory with God.

There are some who claim to be certain that *they* themselves shall be in heaven, but refuse to accept the doctrine of eternal security. By what special dispensation of grace shall they be saved? Are they not resting upon their own stability? Do such people have stronger characters than some weaker brothers who are frequently stumbling? Does salvation make this distinction? It is to be feared that these people

18

do not clearly see that salvation is by grace and grace alone, for the one of strong as well as the one of weak character, and that none are kept because of the slightest human merit.

The principal reason, however, for this volume is that unless one understands and accepts the doctrine of eternal security, one *can not* accept without a great deal of reservation the doctrines of the grace of God. *The whole body of grace truth loses very much of its meaning to those who reject the doctrine of eternal security.*

Some years ago, a minister of national reputation in this country was asked the question: "It makes considerable difference, does it not, how a minister preaches, whether or not he accepts the doctrine of eternal security?" The immediate answer was: "A vast difference."

If there is a vast difference in preaching due to acceptance or rejection of this doctrine, then it surely is important to discuss it. Speaking generally, those who reject this doctrine will in their sermons emphasize works. It becomes: "You must do this and you must not do that." The emphasis is on self and their preaching often causes hearers to question their own salvation. Fear is used as a motive for godly living. Those who accept the doctrine of assurance, tell of what God has done and offer their hearers a finished work of salvation by Jesus Christ. Their appeal to holiness is based on what God has done for the saved one. They magnify the grace of God. Truly there is a vast difference.

WHY USE THE TERM "ETERNAL SECURITY"?

There are those who accept the truth of the eternal security of the believer; but feel that this truth should be taught without reference to that expression, and that the name of the doctrine, because of the resentment against it, should never be used. It is true, because of misrepresentations of the doctrine, that it is wise to follow this course under certain circumstances, especially when it is impossible to deal extensively with the subject. But that does not do away with the need of a frank discussion of the whole subject. There is a great deal of anti-eternal security agitation. Much is preached and written against it. Gross misrepresentations of the doctrine are made. Some of the best Bible teachers and most spiritual Christians in the land are being labeled in certain quarters as "eternal security men" and doors, which otherwise would be open, are closed to them. Thereby congregations, sadly in need of being taught grace truth, are not having the opportunity to hear it. Some of the best Bible teachers are being kept out of summer Bible conferences because of their belief in eternal security, and the young people who so greatly need to know the doctrines of the grace of God are not being taught.

This seems enough to demonstrate the real need of squarely facing this anti-eternal security agitation. That can only be done by using the term eternal security. It is impossible to expose the error of this teaching without using the words that are used so freely.

Some say that the expression eternal security is unbiblical and should not be used. If that is true, so also are the expressions, The Trinity or the Triune God, the Vicarious Death, the Substitutionary Death, Omniscience, Omnipresence, and others that are freely used. These identical words are not in the Bible, but the meaning is there. The Bible teaches that the believer is included in the "eternal purpose" of God (Eph. 3:10, 11); he has "eternal life" (1 John 5:13); his salvation is called "eternal salvation" (Heb. 5:9); he has been redeemed by an "eternal redemption" (Heb. 9:12); he is assured an "eternal inheritance" (Heb. 9:15); and he is called unto "eternal glory" (1 Pet. 5:10). In view of these expressions, it is surely correct to speak of the "eternal security" of the believer for each and every one of these conditions does make him eternally secure.

3

The Issue Clarified

THE STRONG antagonism against the doctrine of eternal security found in some groups is largely due to a misunderstanding of it. There has been much misrepresentation of this doctrine coming from what might be classified as three different sources.

There seems to be a small number of persons who make use of the doctrine as a license to sin. There are not many of these; but those that there are, are being held up as proof that eternal security is something to be shunned. Whether or not such persons have ever been saved is a question that God alone can answer. It is certain, however, that it is not fair to judge a Bible doctrine by the misrepresentations of men who try to use it as a cloak for their wickedness. To point to such men and argue that eternal security is an evil teaching to be shunned is just as reasonable as it would be to hold up a counterfeit United States twenty-dollar bill and insist that because of it, all good twenty-dollar bills should be rejected. When counterfeit bills are found, they are taken out of circulation so as to protect the sound money. Likewise when some one uses the precious doctrine of eternal security as a license, the error should be exposed that the truth might be retained.

There is a second source of information about

eternal security which results in misunderstandings. This presentation of the doctrine is not erroneous, but is unfortunate in that it is only partial. The whole truth is not explained and some of those who hear draw wrong conclusions. This presentation comes from persons, often young people attending either a Bible school or summer Bible conference, who have received the truth of their security in Christ as a new revelation previously unknown to them. Being overjoyed in the assurance that has come to them, after years of uncertainty as to their salvation, they are eager that others should share the same joy and peace into which they have entered. It is regrettable that there should be this incomplete presentation of this comforting doctrine, but who is to blame for that? While it may be a severe charge, it is none the less true that had there been proper teaching of Bible doctrines in the home churches attended by these persons, such faulty presentations could never have been made. Who is to blame?

The third reason, and probably the greatest, for the antagonism to eternal security is because of the misrepresentation of the doctrine by some who are opposed to it. This may not always be intentional, but it is none the less harmful.

Those who oppose the doctrine of eternal security say that this doctrine teaches that one who has been saved can not be lost; it makes no difference how he lives. The emphasis is usually placed upon the last clause. This is what most uninformed Christians in many churches think is being taught as a doctrine, and they naturally resent such teaching. *So do also*

*those who accept and cherish this doctrine. This is
a very unfair and misleading statement. In fact, the
last half is a pure falsehood.*

Those who hold and understand the doctrine
teach that through the infinite sacrifice of His Own
Son, God through the riches of His grace, saves the
one who comes to Him in simple faith; and that
every one that has been redeemed by the blood of
Christ, God, through His own power, shall bring to
glory.

There is a vast difference between these two
statements. The one is on a human plane, the other
is on a divine. The former centers attention on the
believer's life and implies that salvation is dependent thereon. The second centers attention on God's
love and sacrifice and makes salvation dependent
thereon. The first calls attention to the failures of
oneself; the second to God and His infinite power.
The first suggests a license to sin; the second an appeal to holiness. The first temporizes with sin; the
second glorifies God. The first is an appeal to human
reason; the second an acceptance of divine revelation.

It is a dangerous thing to so misrepresent God's
revelation.

LOST OR SAVED

In all disputes, much misunderstanding is cleared
away by a proper understanding of the terms used.
To be lost is that condition before God of every individual member of the human race before he is
saved. This condition is described as "dead in tres-

passes and sins" and "by nature the children of wrath" (Eph. 2:1, 3). Such are under the condemnation of God's holy law. To be saved is to have passed from this state of condemnation and death into a state of eternal life (John 5:24). The lost are under the reign, or power, of sin unto death; the saved are under the reign, or power, of grace unto eternal life. The transfer from the one position to the other is by an act of God and not of man. A more detailed explanation of what it means to be saved is found in Chapter VI. It is in this sense that the words lost and saved are used when it is said that one who has been saved shall not be lost.

Salvation itself is not an outward condition but a heart relationship with God. As a result of it come outward expressions. In the lives of some, these are more manifest than in others. Abraham and Lot are both spoken of in the Bible as justified (saved) men, but there was much more outward evidence of a heart relationship with God in the life of Abraham.

On the other hand, there may be much of what to man appears as evidence of a new life within, which is not that at all. There are many who profess to be Christians, who take part in religious work, or have joined some church, who have never been saved. Going forward in a revival meeting, weeping or passing through emotional periods, does not constitute being saved. These may and sometimes do accompany salvation, but they are not salvation. It is even possible for men to preach in the Name of Christ without having been saved (Matthew 7:22, 23). A moral reformation is not salvation. In fact, it may be quite the opposite because it may be the result of human will power and action and not of God.

Because man judges the outward being and not the heart, there are many mistakes made in judging persons as saved or unsaved. The doctrine of eternal security has nothing to say about this vast number who only give outward show, but who lack the heart relationship with God.

As the salvation of an individual is a matter entirely of divine accomplishment, so also is the security of every one that has been saved. It follows then that man's knowledge of both the fact of salvation and security must primarily come as a revelation from God.

To many, it seems most unreasonable that one who has been saved is not lost because of his sins and failures. It truly is unreasonable, but it is equally unreasonable that God should save one who has sunk to the lowest depths of sin; yea, even a very intellectual and moral person but still a sinner, and raise him to the highest position in glory far above all other creatures of God. But it has pleased God to reveal that fact to man. He has also revealed the fact that He has made provision to keep every one that has thus been saved. *There is but one thing to do: accept that which God has revealed through His Word, however much that may differ from what one has been taught in the past.* In the discussion of this question, then, no such statements as, "We know from our own experience" have any weight. It is only a question: *"What does God say?"*

4

God Says So

THE SIMPLEST evidence in support of the doctrine of eternal security is a large number of Scripture passages which state in plain, unconditional language the facts that can mean nothing else than that all who have been saved are saved for all eternity.

Some of these, in addition to John 10:27-29 already used, are quoted below:

"For God so loved the world, that He gave His only begotten Son, that whosoever believeth in Him should not perish, but have *everlasting life*" (John 3:16).

"Verily, verily, I say unto you, He that heareth My Word, and believeth Him that sent Me, *hath eternal life,* and *cometh not into judgment;* but *hath passed* out of death into life" (John 5:24, R. V.).

"All that the Father giveth Me *shall* come unto Me; and him that cometh to Me I will in no wise cast out" (John 6:37).

"And this is the Father's will Who hath sent Me that of *all* which He hath given Me *I should lose nothing,* but should raise it up again at the last day. And this is the will of Him that sent Me, that everyone which seeth the Son, and believeth on Him, may have everlasting life: and *I shall raise him up* at the last day" (John 6:39, 40).

"But God commendeth His love toward us, in that, while we were yet sinners, Christ died for us. *Much more* then, being now justified by His blood, we *shall be saved from wrath* through Him" (Rom. 5:8, 9).

"There is therefore now no *condemnation* to them which are in Christ Jesus" (Rom. 8:1). The last ten words printed in the Authorized Version have been interpolated. They are not in the Revised Version. Those who use the Swedish Bible will find that they are not in it.

"But if the Spirit of Him that raised up Jesus from the dead dwell in you [and He does dwell in every saved person], He that raised up Christ from the dead *shall* also quicken your mortal bodies by His Spirit that dwelleth in you" (Rom. 8:11).

"For whom He did foreknow He also did *predestinate* to be conformed to the image of His Son. . . . Moreover whom He did predestinate, them He also called; and whom He called, them He also justified: and whom He justified, them He also *glorified*" (Rom. 8:29, 30).

"Who shall lay *anything* to the charge of God's elect? It is God that justifieth. Who is he that condemneth? It is Christ that died, yea rather, that is risen again, Who is even at the right hand of God, Who also maketh intercession for us" (Rom. 8:33, 34). All saved are included in "God's elect." To be lost is to have a charge laid against oneself and to be condemned. God has made provision against both.

"Who [God] shall also confirm you unto the end, that ye be blameless in the day of our Lord Jesus Christ. God is faithful, by Whom ye were called unto the fellowship of His Son Jesus Christ our Lord" (1 Cor. 1:8, 9).

"And as we [all who are saved] have borne the image of the earthy [Adam], we *shall* also bear the image of the heavenly [Jesus Christ] (1 Cor. 15:49).

"Being confident of this very thing, that He Who hath begun a good work in you [all who have been saved] *will perform it until the day of Jesus Christ*" (Phil. 1:6).

"For ye [who are saved] are dead and *your life is hid with Christ in God*. When Christ, Who is our life, shall appear, then *shall ye also* appear with Him in glory" (Col. 3:3, 4).

"And the Lord shall deliver me from every evil work, and will *preserve me unto His heavenly Kingdom:* to Whom be glory for ever and ever" (2 Tim. 4:18).

"Who are kept by the power of God through faith unto salvation ready to be revealed in the last time" (1 Pet. 1:5).

"Beloved, now are we the sons [born ones] of God, and it doth not yet appear what we shall be: but *we know* that, when He shall appear, we shall be like Him; for we shall see Him as He is" (1 John 3:2). Anyone who can at this moment, or at any moment say: I am a child of God, I am saved, can also say, I *know* that I shall be like Him. There is not the slightest trace of anything conditional in this verse.

These passages are unquestionably written to, or about, the saved of this age. There is nothing in the context of any of them to qualify their meaning. They are in nonfigurative language which does not call for explanation.

If these passages do not declare that the one who is saved shall remain saved unto the end and share the glory of Christ in His heavenly Kingdom, then words are without any certain meaning.

Surely God says that the saved one is eternally secure.

5

Eternal Security and the Doctrines
of the Grace of God

IN THE preceding Chapter, a sufficiently large number of Scripture passages were quoted to support
the truth of eternal security, leaving no room for
any reasonable doubt. But there is even more certain evidence to support this truth, if any one part of
God's Word can be said to be more sure than any
other.

It must be admitted by all that *the doctrines of
the grace of God are a related body of truth, each
part of which harmonizes perfectly with each and
every other part. There must be no contradictions
between the various doctrines and no confusion as
to their meanings, for God is the God of order and
not of confusion.*

*The fundamental question then is: Does the truth
of eternal security harmonize and fit in with all the
doctrines of the grace of God, or does the declaration that one who has been saved can be lost do so?*
As these two positions are contradictory to each
other, only one of them can be so harmonized. *That
position which can be harmonized must then be*

accepted as fundamentally correct and the other discarded. This is of far greater weight than the quotation of separate Scripture passages to support the one side or the other. In fact, *it must be conceded that, if it can be established that the one position is in harmony with all the doctrines of grace and the other is in discord with them, it becomes imperative to interpret individual verses in harmony with the conclusions from a study of the doctrines.* Certainly no passage can be interpreted so as to build a doctrine that is out of harmony with the great body of grace truth.

It is the purpose of this section to show that the truth of eternal security is in perfect accord with the truths of the grace of God. It will be shown that the doctrine of eternal security and all the others either stand or fall together. Each and everyone of these doctrines requires the acceptance of the truth of eternal security for a full and clear acceptance thereof. Thus the doctrine of eternal security might be said to be the keystone of the arch of the doctrines of grace, or it might be likened to the warp of a fabric of which the other doctrines of grace are the woof. Take out the doctrine of eternal security and the arch falls, or the fabric falls apart.

Those who support the position that one who has been saved can be lost never put their position to this test. In fact they are not known to quote any doctrine of grace to support their position. They rest their case on individual Scripture passages, the interpretations of which are questionable or have actually been read into these passages by themselves and often entirely contrary to the context in which they are found. This, however, will be discussed in a later section.

It will not only be shown that the doctrine of eternal security is in harmony with the doctrines of grace, but it will also be shown that the opposing view makes these doctrines void and meaningless.

It will be seen from the discussion of the different doctrines that eternal security is not a separate doctrine, but is actually an inseparable part of each of the doctrines of the grace of God and therefore it seems more exact to speak of the "truth" or "fact" of eternal security than the doctrine of eternal security.

What follows is not offered as an exhaustive study of all of the doctrines, nor is it all of any one doctrine. What is claimed for it is, that it calls attention to those parts of a large number of doctrines which have a bearing on the doctrine of eternal security. It makes no claim to be a scholarly theological discussion of these doctrines.

6

Saved by Grace Through Faith

"FOR BY grace are ye saved through faith; and that not of yourselves: it is the gift of God: not of works, lest any man should boast" (Eph. 2:8, 9). This passage deals with the past tense of salvation. It is salvation from the guilt, penalty and condemnation of sin. *It has already been fully accomplished*. It is *not a process* that is being carried on to be perfected at a later time. In its present tense, salvation is from the power of sin and is a process. In its future tense, salvation will be from the presence of sin and will be accomplished "in a moment in the twinkling of an eye."

Salvation, to use the words of another, is in no sense a probation. To be saved by grace, to some, seems to mean to be placed in such a relation to God that at the end of the earthly life, one enters glory, provided, however, that one has been faithful to God and has lived according to certain moral standards. It is not stated as definitely as this, but that is a very fair statement of the meaning of salvation to be gleaned from a great deal of present day preaching.

The doctrinal epistles tell of a great many things that are true of the one who has been saved. These

are all spoken of as being fully accomplished. There
is no mention of growth or development of any one
of them. They are always considered as being final.
The following is only an incomplete list of these
things. It is not necessary to enumerate all in order
to prove that the one who has been "saved" is in an
unalterable condition. Some of these are more fully
discussed in later chapters.

The saved person has been redeemed from under
the law (Gal. 4:5), and the curse of the law (Gal.
3:13), by an eternal redemption (Heb. 9:12). He is
dead to the law (Rom. 7:4), and shall not come into
condemnation (John 5:24, Rom. 8:1). He is reconciled to God (2 Cor. 5:18), and is at peace with
Him (Col. 1:20). He is justified (Rom. 5:1), and
all trespasses have been forgiven (Col. 2:13). He
has been delivered from the power of darkness and
translated into the kingdom of the Son of God (Col.
1:13). He has been born again of incorruptible seed
(1 Pet. 1:23); is a son of God (John 1:12); and has
eternal life (John 5:24). He is a new creature (2
Cor. 5:17). He is perfected forever (Heb. 10:14);
is complete in Christ (Col. 2:10); and has been accepted of God (Eph. 1:6). He has been born of the
Spirit (John 3:6); baptized by the Spirit (1 Cor.
12:13); is indwelt by the Spirit Who abides forever
(John 14:16, 17); and has been sealed by the Spirit
until the day of redemption (Eph. 4:30). He has
become the object of God's love (Eph. 2:4), of His
grace (Rom. 6:14), of His power (Eph. 1:19), and
of His faithfulness (1 Cor. 1:9). He is a citizen of

heaven (Eph. 2:19 and Phil. 3:20 R. V.); is seated with Christ in the heavenly places (Eph. 2:6); and is already glorified (Rom. 8:30).

All of the above, and more too, God says of the one who has been saved. *Before the one who has been saved can be lost, everyone of these things must be made void. Is that possible? God's Word is absolutely silent as to any such possibility. This should be final, for it is only through His revelation that these facts are known to man. It could only, by a similar revelation, be known that they are subject to change if that were possible.*

Can one who has been redeemed by an eternal redemption be brought back into bondage? Can one who is dead to the law be made alive to it? Can one within the Kingdom of God be taken out of it? Can one born again of incorruptible seed and having eternal life die? Can one that has been perfected forever be found imperfect? Can one that is complete in Christ become incomplete? *These are eternal in their very nature, and therefore are unalterable.*

Only when all of these questions can be answered in the affirmative, can one who has been saved be said to be lost. *The burden of proof rests squarely upon those who say that one who has been saved can be lost to show that these things can be made void.* To many, it is a light matter to say that one who has been saved can be lost, but how many understand the full import of that statement?

IT IS BY GRACE

Grace excludes all merit on the part of the one who is the object thereof. Therefore to be saved by grace cannot take into account any merit in the saved one, either before, at the time of, or after the time he is saved. Furthermore, grace is shown toward the one who is actually guilty. "While we were yet sinners, Christ died for us" (Rom. 5:8). Therefore demerit does not hinder the operation of grace, nor can it set aside that which grace has accomplished. In fact, demerit is the occasion for grace to accomplish its work.

The conclusion drawn from this is that that which God has done by the operation of His grace is unalterable. And this is exactly what God says about grace. ". . . it is of faith, that it might be by grace; to the end that the promise might be sure to all the seed" (Rom. 4:16).

Thus *to be saved by grace is to be unalterably saved and that for all eternity*. The saved one cannot be anything but eternally secure.

THROUGH FAITH

There is no merit in faith. "It is of faith that it might be by grace." If there were the slightest merit in faith, it could not be a channel through which grace could work. It would be a counter agent to grace which, as has been seen, by its very nature excludes merit on the part of the saved one. Faith does not only exclude the thought of merit, it actually includes the idea of helplessness and hopelessness. In faith one calls upon another to do that which one is unable to do for oneself. A child in the family is sick and near death. The family physician is called. In so doing the parents confess their own inability to deal with the illness and express their confidence in the doctor. There is no merit in calling the doctor. Their faith in the doctor merely gives him the opportunity to work.

The object of the sinner's faith is Christ. He did not come into this world to *help* men to be saved. He came to *save* that which was lost—that which was beyond all human help. As Savior, He came to give His life as a ransom—to die, and thereby take upon Himself the judgment for sin.

Jesus gave a clear illustration of what faith in Him means. He said to Nicodemus: "As Moses lifted up the serpent in the wilderness, even so must the Son of man be lifted up: that whosoever believeth in Him should not perish, but have eternal life" (John 3:14, 15). The Israelite in the wilderness showed his faith by looking on the serpent of brass that hung on the pole (see Num. 21:5-9). In this one act of faith was expressed a confession of sin and utter helplessness and an acknowledgment that God's provision was his *only* hope. He did not understand the significance of the serpent, nor why it was made of brass. He did not analyze his faith to see if it was sufficient. He did not question the intensity of his look. He surely claimed no merit for looking. There were just two things in his mind: his own absolute hopelessness and the sufficiency of God's provision. And this is all that there is to that faith through which the lost are saved. There is no power in faith that contributes to salvation.

And yet there are men who discuss faith as something which is meritorious on the part of the believer. Some even say that faith is a work. This is impossible for salvation is through faith and "not of works." Sometimes one hears sinners invited to come to the cross and lay their sin burden there. If this were possible, it might be contended that faith is a work, but even this is impossible. No person can take the sin burden off of himself. The sin burden must always rest upon a person and it stays on the sinner until it is taken and placed upon Christ and that can be done only by God. *"The Lord* hath laid on Him the iniquity of us all" (Isa. 53:6). If man is totally incapable of doing anything to remove the sin burden from himself, he is much more incapable of contributing anything to the doing of all of the things already mentioned as being true of the one who is saved.

Through faith (that is the acknowledgment of one's own utter helplessness and hopelessness and the casting of one's self upon God's provision) God is able to act in grace. That is the meaning of: "It is of faith that it might be by grace." That is also the meaning of: "As many as received Him, to them gave He power to become the sons of God" (John 1:12).

*The meaning of faith then, as well as the meaning
of grace, excludes every possible vestige of human
merit. If every possible vestige of human merit is
excluded, then man's acts, apart from accepting the
Savior, are not related to salvation and thus no act
of man or demerit of man can cause him to be taken
out of the condition of being saved. But this is exactly what is argued by those who contend against
the doctrine of eternal security.*

The fact that saving faith is an act and not a
process must not be construed to mean that there is
no further need for faith. "The just shall live by
faith" (Rom. 1:17). God has much more in view for
the saved person than being saved from the guilt,
penalty and condemnation of sin and into the Kingdom of His dear Son, even as much as that means.
He desires that those who have themselves been
saved shall bear "more fruit" and "much fruit." This
is to live a Spirit-directed life that shows others the
way of salvation. That is the life that the just (one
who has been justified through one act of faith)
shall live by the faith principle of confessing one's
own inability and full dependence upon God.

AND THAT NOT OF YOURSELVES

God does not trust man to see his own absolute
lack of merit merely through the meaning of the
words grace and faith, for *to know his own lack of
merit and absolute worthlessness in relation to God
is man's hardest lesson to learn.* So God adds the
definite statement "not of yourselves." Again, no

human merit can contribute to salvation. *God is very zealous to have it known that He and He only is responsible for man's salvation.* And yet well meaning, sincere Christians will insist on some "must" or "musts" on the part of man in order for him to remain saved.

But there is a further meaning to the words "not of yourselves." The word "yourselves" is addressed to men who in themselves are fallible, who are finite and who are incapable of good as God judges goodness. If salvation were by such, it would be faulty, it would be limited in extent and duration, it would not be good and acceptable unto God.

If it were part of God and part of self, as it must be if the slightest degree of merit or demerit of man were taken into account, it would still be faulty, limited and unacceptable to God, to whatever extent man's merit or demerit be taken into account. There would somewhere be one weak link in the chain. As the strength of the chain is the strength of its weakest link, there cannot be the slightest link of human merit in the salvation chain that binds the believer to God. But there is no weak link in that chain, because it is "not of yourselves" and therefore the believer is eternally secure.

Every argument against the eternal security of the believer is based on the human element. As God definitely and clearly excludes all human element in salvation, every one of these arguments is thereby ruled out.

IT IS THE GIFT OF GOD

Salvation is a gift from God. Again, and for the fourth time, all thought of merit is excluded, for a gift is not a gift in the full sense of the word if it is in exchange for even the slightest thing. And again, the fact that salvation is said to be a gift from God, makes it unchangeable, for the "gifts . . . of God are without repentance" (Rom. 11:29).

This gift is "*of God.*" It is not only given by God, it is also prepared by Him. All of the aforementioned things that are true of every believer are provided by God and are thereby perfect and acceptable to Him. "They are made to stand on the unchanging person and merit of the eternal Son of God" (Lewis Sperry Chafer in his book, *Salvation*), for they are all "through Christ" and because of His merit. They are therefore of infinite and eternal value in the sight of God. The one who has received the gift of salvation must then be eternally secure. *To say that one who has been saved can be lost is to say that there can be failure in these things which are of God. That implies deficiency in the merit of Christ and in the power of God working through Him.* Dare anyone say that that is possible?

NOT OF WORKS LEST ANY MAN SHOULD BOAST

Works and grace are said to be mutually exclusive of each other. "And if by grace, then is it no more works: otherwise grace is no more grace. But if it be of works, then is it no more grace: otherwise work is no more work" (Rom. 11:6). Therefore, as salvation is by grace, all that in any way might be works, whether it be to will or to do, is excluded.

Works are also the opposite of faith. That which is of works is of man's effort and is meritorious to him. By works man confesses his own ability and displays confidence in self. Israel did this at Sinai when they answered Moses: "All that the Lord hath spoken we will do" (Ex. 19:8). On the contrary, as has been seen, faith confesses one's own disability and dependence upon another for that which is to be done.

Thus where there are works there is boasting of man, but where it is through faith, there is no boasting of man. Therefore salvation is "not of works lest any man should boast." "Where is boasting then? It is excluded. By what law? of works? Nay: but by the law of faith" (Rom. 3:27). This is so "that no flesh shall glory in His Presence" (1 Cor. 1:29).

Thus there can be nothing—absolutely nothing—bearing on the salvation of man from the guilt, penalty and condemnation of sin and into the glorious Kingdom of the Son of God that can in the slightest degree be of works by the saved one himself. This is all excluded for the very purpose of excluding boasting by man.

TO THE PRAISE OF THE GLORY OF HIS GRACE

God does not save man because of any value in man or because man is too good to be lost; for there is no goodness in man, "they are together become unprofitable; there is none that doeth good, no not one" (Rom. 3:12). God saves men so "that in the ages to come He might shew the exceeding riches of His grace in His kindness toward us through Christ Jesus" (Eph. 2:7).

The supreme purpose of God in salvation is: "To the praise of the glory of His grace" (Eph. 1:6 and 2:7). In eternity those who are saved shall sing a new song saying: "Thou wast slain, and hast redeemed us to God by Thy blood." There shall be no discord in that song. Here on earth there is a definitely discordant note every time someone says that the saved one must not sin, must continue in faith, must hold out, must do this and must not do that in order to remain saved. The praise is not all given to the blood. But these notes shall not be heard there, for they are of the flesh and no flesh shall glory in His Presence. To Him only and to the glory of His grace shall be all the praise.

7

The Gift of the Son of God

THE ONLY ground upon which God does anything for man is the gift of His own Son. "God so loved the world that He gave His only begotten Son" (John 3:16). It was while "we were yet sinners, Christ died for us" (Rom. 5:8). This offer is to all, but only to "as many as received Him . . . gave He power to become the sons of God" (John 1:12).

To those who accept the Son as a gift, God gives everything else that is needed by a child of His. "He that spared not His own Son, but delivered Him up for us all, how shall He not with Him also freely give us all things?" (Rom. 8:32). The fact that the Son was delivered up thus becomes of *infinite* value to every one that receives Him, for *all things* are given and received with Him. *The "all things" include every possible thing that the believer's spiritual welfare might require under every conceivable condition. It is nothing less than a divinely perfect provision for the one who has the Son.* This must include a provision against being lost.

There are some things that are specifically mentioned in the Bible as being gifts from God. They are: eternal life (Rom. 6:23), The Holy Spirit (Acts 8:17) and Righteousness (Rom. 5:16, 17).

45

As long as a person has the Son and with Him these other gifts, he is saved.

Those who teach that a saved person can be lost necessarily teach that these gifts can be lost. They say God takes the eternal life back to Himself or that the Holy Spirit will depart from one who has received Him. These are man's words, not God's.

What does God say? He says "the gifts . . . of God are without repentance" (Rom. 11:29). *If God says that He does not repent having given a gift, it is contradicting Him and making Him a liar to say that He takes His gifts back.* No. One who has received, as a free gift from God, first His Son and with Him righteousness, eternal life, and the Holy Spirit and all other things, will always have these throughout all eternity and is eternally secure.

Still there are some who prefer to reason rather than accept the finality of God's Word. They say: "Oh, yes, God does not take back His gifts, but a man can throw them away." *Where is the Scripture proof for this?* The Bible says that the Holy Spirit abides forever (John 14:16). Can He be thrown away? The gift of Righteousness is a matter of God's own accounting (Rom. 4:24). Has man access to God's books so he can change them? Can eternal life be thrown away? Man can throw away his physical life by committing suicide. But that life is a mortal one. Can suicide be committed when the life is eternal?

God has given these infinite gifts to men that He should be praised for them. Paul says "Thanks be unto God for His unspeakable gift" (2 Cor. 9:15). *There is no thanks given to God by teaching that God takes His gifts back or that they can be thrown away.*

Thus the doctrine of eternal security is inseparably related to the teachings concerning the gift of the Son.

8

The Substitutionary Death of Christ

THE WAGES of sin is death" (Rom. 6:23), "The soul that sinneth it shall die" (Ezek. 18:20). This is God's law. It is far more unalterable than the laws of the Medes and Persians. God's own righteousness demands that His law be held inviolate; the penalty of the law must be enforced. There can be no exception made. Not one sin can He overlook, even the smallest. God, sitting as Judge, would be unjust if He did not impose the death penalty of His law upon all.

The voice of His law has stopped every mouth and declared everyone guilty before Him (Rom. 3:19). There is no human means of escape. But God has provided a means whereby He might remain just and yet deliver the sinner from the death penalty of his sins.

The sentence has been imposed. Sinning humanity stood guilty before the Judge, awaiting the execution of the sentence. But before the execution took place the gates of heaven were opened. The Son of God was sent forth. He was given a body which was in the *form* of sinful flesh. But He was not sinful. He "did no sin, neither was guile found in His mouth" (1 Pet. 2:22). He was as "a lamb without blemish and without spot" (1 Pet. 1:19).

The centurion was right when he said: "Certainly this was a righteous Man" (Luke 23:47).

Because He was sinless, He was not under the condemnation of the law. But He presented Himself to God the Judge to ransom those who were under that condemnation, and paid the death penalty in their behalf. Thereby those who accept Him as the One Who paid the penalty of the law in their stead shall not die, but live.

He, Himself, said that just this was the purpose of His coming into the world. "The Son of man is come . . . to save that which was lost" (Luke 19:10). "The Son of man came . . . to give His life a ransom for many" (Matt. 20:28). "I am come that they (the sheep) might have life" (John 10:10).

This giving of His life was a voluntary act on His part. He said, "No man taketh it from Me, but I lay it down of Myself" (John 10:18).

God the Judge accepted His offering and "laid upon Him the iniquity of us all" (Isa. 53:6). "Him Who knew no sin He made to be sin on our behalf; that we might become the righteousness of God in Him" (2 Cor. 5:21 R. V.).

He "bare our sins in His own body on the tree" (1 Pet. 2:24). "For Christ also hath once suffered for sins, the just for the unjust, that He might bring us to God" (1 Pet. 3:18).

In that great event that took place on Calvary's hill, God, the righteous Judge, sitting in judgment, took the sins of sinning mankind and laid them upon His own Son. Then He carried out the execution of

the judgment upon Him. Everyone standing before
God as a guilty sinner who will acknowledge this
death of the Son of God as paying the penalty for
his sins is immediately declared by God as having
fully satisfied the demands of the law and is free
from its penalty. Because Christ died on his behalf, he is then in the sight of the law as one dead.
He is dead to the law and thenceforth the law, as
the *only* ministration of death, has nothing to do
with him. Paul states this fact clearly and repeatedly: " . . . my brethren, ye also are become dead
to the law by the body of Christ" (Rom. 7:4). And
again: "But now we are delivered from the law, that
being dead wherein we were held" (Rom. 7:6). And
still again: "For I through the law am dead to the
law" (Gal. 2:19).

The substitutionary death of Christ then means
that He was put to death in the place of the sinner to
satisfy God's law that demands that "the soul that
sinneth it shall die." *Thus the death sentence has
not only been imposed; the sinner who believes in
Christ, has in the Person of Christ been executed
and from thenceforth he cannot be condemned by
the law for he is dead in its sight. Thus one who has
been saved by being ransomed by the death of
Christ cannot be lost.*

> "Payment God will not twice demand,
> Once from my bleeding Surety's hand
> And then again from me."

Some are able to accept this truth insofar as it
affects sins committed prior to the time they were

saved, but believe that sins committed afterward may cause one to be lost. To such there are several answers.

In the first place, did Christ die for their sins at the moment they accepted Him? No, it was almost nineteen hundred years before a single sin had been committed by them. When He died He did so for the sins of the whole human race which have been committed over a period of six thousand years. Therefore it cannot be a question of the time sin was committed.

Again, it must be remembered that God does not work according to the calendar. When He looks at the life of any particular individual it is not as a biography of successive events, but as a composite portrait of sinful and righteous acts. This must be so, for He saw everyone before the foundation of the world, before time was. In taking an individual's sins then, and placing them on Christ, whether it was those of a saint of the Old Testament or of one living today, He considered the entire sin element of that life and passed judgment upon it. *As far as the penalty of God's holy law and the demands of His righteousness are concerned, the sin question is settled once and for all the very moment an individual believes that Christ paid the penalty in his place.*

If one who has been saved and is dead to the law by the body of Christ could be lost, then it would be possible to put to death the same person twice. This is impossible. Therefore, to say that it is possible for one who has been saved to be lost, is to deny the value of the substitutionary death of Christ.

But God does not leave this question open. He has given the most definite assurance that those who have been saved by the death of Christ shall be eternally saved. He says: "But God commendeth His love toward us, in that, while we were yet sinners, Christ died for us. *Much more* then, being now justified by His blood, we *shall* be saved from wrath through Him" (Rom. 5:8, 9).

9

Redemption

B ECAUSE "THE law worketh wrath" (Rom. 4:15), one who is under the law is subject to the wrath of God.

"What things soever the law saith, it saith to them who are under the law: that every mouth may be stopped, and all the world may become guilty before God" (Rom. 3:19). The law is the ministration of death and of condemnation (2 Cor. 3:7, 9). Therefore, one who is under the law is guilty before God and condemned to death.

Therefore, the one who is under the law is lost.

A saved person has been redeemed from the curse of the law (Gal. 3:13) and from under the law (Gal. 4:5). He is no longer under the law, but under grace (Rom. 6:14).

Redemption was accomplished by the death penalty being borne by Jesus Christ instead of by the sinner. Thus execution by substitute, as explained in the last preceding chapter, has been actually carried out. In the sight of the law, the guilty sinner is dead—dead to the law (Rom. 7:4) and therefore free from it.

If one who is saved is to be lost, it is necessary to return him into the state of being under the law. As he was freed from the law by payment of the death penalty, he can be brought back under it only by undoing the execution of his substitute. Until that is done, the law can have nothing to say to him. Therefore the payment by Christ of the death penalty of the law on behalf of every sinner that comes to Him demands the acceptance of the doctrine of the eternal security of the believer.

Redemption is said to be: "not with corruptible things—but with the precious blood of Christ, as of a Lamb without blemish and without spot." *This redemption price can never lose its value, for it is incorruptible. It is infinite* in its value, for it is the blood of the infinite Christ. *It is perfect* for He was without spot or blemish. And *it is precious. An incorruptible, infinite, perfect and precious redemption price insures an unchangeable, infinite, complete redemption.* And such the redemption of the believer is. "By His own blood He [Christ] entered in once into the holy place, having obtained eternal redemption for us" (Heb. 9:12). Inasmuch as the redemption of the one who has been saved from under the law is eternal, he cannot again come under the law and be condemned to death by it. He can, therefore, not be lost. *Eternal redemption and eternal security are one and mean the same thing. There can be no doctrine of eternal redemption without the fact of eternal security.*

As conclusive as all of this is, it is not all that God has done to make the redemption of the saved one absolutely certain. Redemption is not only *from* something, it is also to God (Rev. 5:9). Everyone who is saved has been "bought" (1 Cor. 7:23) by Christ, and the transaction has been sealed and witnessed.

After an individual has, through faith, accepted Christ as his Redeemer, he is sealed by the Holy Spirit and is also given Him as a witness to what has been done. This sealing is "until the redemption of the purchased possession" (Eph. 1:14). The seal is legal evidence of a consummated purchase, and is proof of ownership.

A beautiful illustration of the use of the seal is found in the story of the purchase by Jeremiah of a field from Hanameel, his uncle's son. The transaction was sealed according to law; and witnessed and the purchase price, seventeen shekels of silver, was weighed in the balances. Then Jeremiah gave the evidence of the purchase, both that which was sealed according to law, and that which was open (i. e., witnessed) and gave them to Baruch to be put in an earthen vessel. The field then was Jeremiah's by purchase. (See Jeremiah 32:8-14.)

That incident in the life of Jeremiah is a beautiful picture of the sealing by the Holy Spirit. The transfer of the field to Jeremiah was a legal transaction. So also Christ becomes owner of every believer through a legal transaction. Natural man is under the law and condemned to death. In Christ is vested the right of redemption. He paid the redemption price, not shekels of silver, the redemption money of the temple, but His own precious blood to satisfy the requirements of the law. On behalf of everyone who believes, evidence is subscribed and sealed. The seal is the Holy Spirit. In addition thereto, a witness is taken. This also is the Holy Spirit (Rom. 8:15, 16). These evidences are then placed in an earthen vessel—the believer's body, where they continue until the redemption of the purchased possession is consummated.

A sealed and witnessed transaction is unalterable. It is final. It is irrevocable. The one who has been bought from under the bondage of sin and the condemnation of the law cannot be returned to that state. The seal is effective throughout the entire earthly life of the believer. To deny the eternal security of the believer is to reject the value of the seal and witness of the Holy Spirit.

Thus the fact of eternal security is as vital to the doctrine of redemption as life is to the body. Take life away from the body and it is useless, it returns to the dust. Take security out of the doctrine of redemption and its life-giving power is gone. The doctrine of Redemption demands the doctrine of eternal security.

10

The New Birth

UNFORTUNATELY, COMPARATIVELY few Christians really understand what it means to be "born again." "Ye must be born again" is a favorite sermon topic. But why is it such a rare thing to hear a simple exposition of what the new birth means and what takes place when one is born again? Those that deny the eternal security of the believer do not explain it.

The new birth is as real as the first birth. The Lord Jesus Christ said to Nicodemus: "That which is born of the flesh is flesh; and that which is born of the Spirit is spirit" (John 3:6).

The word birth, when used literally, always means the coming into existence of a new life which has the same nature as the parents. When a wolf, or a sheep, is born, there is a new life which has the wolf nature or the sheep nature, as the case may be. When a child is born into the world, a new life comes into existence. This life has a human nature which is sinful. It is therefore subject to death. This is the birth that Jesus called "of the flesh" and the result of that birth is flesh. This life cannot change its nature. It is as grass that withers, and as a flower that falls away (1 Pet. 1:24). *To be saved does not mean that this life which is born of the flesh is changed or made over.* This cannot happen, for its nature cannot be changed. That is the condition that makes the new birth imperative. The only thing God could do with the flesh was to judge it, and the judgment resulted in condemnation and execution (Rom. 8:3; Gal. 2:19; Rom. 6:6).

The new birth is a birth of the Spirit. It is to be "born, not of blood, nor of the will of the flesh, nor of the will of man, but of God" (John 1:13). *It is the coming into being of a new, divine life which has the incorruptible and immortal (not subject to death) nature of God.* Of the new birth Peter writes: "Being born again, not of corruptible seed, but of incorruptible, by the Word of God, which liveth and abideth for ever" (1 Pet. 1:23). This seed not only lives forever, but it has also been revealed that it *remains* (1 John 3:9) in the one who is born of God. Such a life must be eternal and that is what Jesus said it is (John 3:16). That life which is eternal cannot die. All who are born of incorruptible seed have an incorruptible nature and have eternal life. It is impossible for such to be lost for that would mean the corruption of the divine nature and the death of that which cannot die.

By the new birth, one who has already been born into the human race is born into the spiritual realm, that is, the Kingdom of God. This is the only way to see or enter into that realm (John 3:3, 5).

Not a single individual who has been born into the human race has been able to remove himself from it. Many have committed suicide, but all that they have done is to shorten the days of their earthly existence. Their existence still continues, on and on and on into the eternity of the future. How some men would like to obliterate themselves entirely from the human race! Yet they cannot because of the inexorable law: once born a man, always a man.

And yet some teach that one who has been saved can be lost by willfully going away from God. This is the same as saying that one who has been born into the Kingdom of God can, by his own will, separate himself from the spiritual realm. By analogy with the human race, this is impossible. The burden of proof rests heavily upon those who so teach to produce Scripture passages which show unmistakably that this is possible. None has as yet produced such proof. In fact, these teachers do not attempt to prove this and similar statements by quoting Scripture. They simply make the statements and their hearers or readers who are untutored in Bible doctrine accept them at face value.

Those who reject the eternal security of the believer, pervert the doctrine of the new birth (either consciously or unconsciously) by believing that eternal life is received first at the end of the present earthly life. In the meantime the "saved person" might lose his chance of receiving it. This is a widely accepted error. Eternal life, however, is an ever present possession of all who are born again, from the very moment they were so born.

Jesus said: "Verily, verily, I say unto you, He that heareth My Word, and believeth Him that sent Me, *hath eternal* life, and cometh not into judgment [condemnation] but hath passed out of death into life" (John 5:24 R. V.).

All of this is accomplished in a moment when the sinner, by believing, accepts Christ and is born again. The word "hath" does not mean "is receiving" nor "will receive." It means already possessed. Three times in this verse, the unending nature of the believer's life is stated: (1) hath eternal life, (2) cometh not into judgment and (3) is passed from death into life. Notice also that Jesus calls special attention to the fact that He is authority for the statement. He says "I say unto you." And that is not all. He emphasizes it with the strongest expression He ever used: "Verily, verily." What finality of expression is used here by the Lord Jesus Christ!

And yet it is possible to be so blinded by the teaching that one who has been saved can be lost, that this cannot be understood. At the close of a session of a Bible class in which the truth of the believer's present possession of eternal life had been pointed out, one of the members said: "I *can't* believe that we now have eternal life, for that would be eternal security and I *won't* believe that." Not all are as honest in expressing their position as was this person, but their minds are just as closed to the truth. They *cannot see the truth,* because of adherence to a false teaching which absolutely contradicts it.

Those who teach that one who has been saved can be lost, also teach that such an one can be saved again. To be saved means to be born again. If it were possible to be lost, that would mean the death of the life resulting from the new birth. Then to be saved a second time it becomes necessary to be born again a second time. With some, it would be a third, fourth, fifth time and so on indefinitely. Is there any Scripture to support such juggling of the simple meaning of the word birth?

Just how far astray the rejection of the doctrine of eternal security will bring men is seen in connection with the doctrine of the new birth. To accept "new birth" as meaning a new eternal life as real as the physical life received by the first birth makes their position untenable. So the new birth is called a "symbol of salvation." This precious, basic, vital doctrine is made figurative language. Its force is lost. Its clear meaning is lost. The Word of God has been made void.

11

The New Creation in Christ Jesus

THERE IS a doctrine that is very little known and still less taught that is very closely related to the doctrine of the New Birth. It is the "new creation in Christ Jesus."

He who is saved is *"created* in Christ Jesus" (Eph. 2:10). "In Christ Jesus neither circumcision availeth anything, nor uncircumcision, but a *new creature"* (Gal. 6:15). This creation takes the place of the old creation in the first Adam. "If any man be in Christ Jesus, he is a *new creature*: old things are passed away; behold, all things are become new" (2 Cor. 5:17). This new creation is "the new man, which after God is *created* in righteousness and true holiness" (Eph. 4:24).

The new man is the born-again man, the one born of the spirit, as distinguished from the old man, or carnal man, the one born of the flesh. The old man has a corrupt human nature, with inborn tendency to evil. The new man is partaker of a divine nature and life and *is in no sense the old man made over, or improved.* (See Dr. Scofield's Reference notes to Eph. 4:24 and Rom. 6:6.)

God created Adam in His own likeness (Gen. 5:1, 2). Afterward, "Adam . . . begat a son in his own likeness, after his image and called his name Seth"

(Gen. 5:3). Thus is stated the beginning of the generations of the human race.

But something had happened in the interval between the second and third verses. Adam through sin had lost the likeness of God. When Seth was begotten in Adam's "own likeness, after his own image," it was not in the original likeness to God but it was in the likeness of the sinful Adam. And, as it was said of Adam "and he died," so it was also said of Seth—"and he died." The observant reader will find the following formula throughout the chapter: "And all the days of . . . were . . . years: and he died." There is but one exception, Enoch, of whom it is not said, "And he died." Enoch who was "translated that he should not see death" (Heb. 11:5), is a type of those saints who are to be translated when Christ comes for His Church.

And ever since, that same formula has applied to man. Every descendant of Adam from Cain and Seth down to the present day, has been born in the likeness and after the image of Adam, with a sinful nature and subject to death. There is absolutely no escape from this condition. Therefore, "Through one man sin entered into the world [humanity], and death through sin; and so death passed unto all men, for that all sinned" (Rom. 5:12 R. V.). Thus "by the offence of one, judgment came upon all men" (Rom. 5:18).

The words which are written large over the first creation, that of which Adam is the federal head, are —"SIN HATH REIGNED UNTO DEATH." That condition is unalterable, for God had commanded Adam not to eat of the fruit of the tree of good and evil and had made death the penalty for disobedience. This means death in its fullest significance, physical death, spiritual death and the second death which is the final everlasting separation of the body, soul and spirit from God. God's commandment has been broken and the penalty cannot be avoided.

To be lost in this first creation is to be dead in trespasses and sins.

When the Son of God became flesh and came into the world, He dwelt among men of the old creation. But He was not of it. He was not of the seed of Adam, but of the seed of the woman. He was conceived by the Holy Ghost. Therefore, He did not possess Adam's sinful nature. He was full of truth (John 1:14). He was in the *likeness* of sinful flesh (Rom. 8:3), but no sin was in Him.

Then through infinite love, He identified Himself with the first creation and took upon Himself the guilt thereof. He was the Lamb of God which taketh away the sin of the world. As a result, He tasted death for every man (Heb. 2:9).

But God raised Him up, "having loosed the pains of death: because it was not possible that He should be holden of it" (Acts 2:24). He arose victorious over death. The Son of God? Yes, but also the Son of man. With His resurrection there was a new creation raised by God out of the death of the old. All who are saved are quickened together with Christ in this resurrection. "But God . . . even when we were dead in sins, hath quickened us together with Christ, (by grace ye are saved) and hath raised us up together, and made us sit together in heavenly places in Christ Jesus" (Eph. 2:4-6).

As the first creation has one man as its federal head, so also has the new, the man Jesus Christ (Rom. 5:15). The first creation received its sinful nature from its federal head, Adam. The new creation receives its righteous nature from its federal head, the man Jesus Christ, for "by the obedience of One, many shall be made righteous" (Rom. 5:19). *In each case, the nature of the creation depends upon the act of the head. It does not depend upon the acts of those that issue from those heads.*

As the unalterable law of the first is Sin unto death, so the law of the new is GRACE REIGNS THROUGH RIGHTEOUSNESS UNTO ETERNAL LIFE. This law of the new creation is even more unalterable than that of the first creation. "For if by one man's offence, death reigned by one: *much more* they which receive abundance of grace and of the gift of righteousness shall reign in life by One, Jesus Christ" (Rom. 5:17). Since the head cannot be condemned (Rom. 6:9, 10), the members of the new creation cannot be condemned.

To be saved is to be in the new creation under the law of righteousness unto eternal life. To be lost is to be in the first creation under the law of sin unto death. If one who has been saved can be lost, it must be possible to bring him back into his original position in the old creation. That is impossible. To say

that this could happen would contradict Jesus' own
words: "He that heareth My words and believeth on
Him that sent Me, . . shall not come into condemnation; but is passed from death unto life"
(John 5:24). Furthermore, for everyone that is in
the new creation, the old has *passed away* (2 Cor.
5:17). There *can be no return* to it.

To say that a saved person, one who has been
quickened together with Christ, can be lost is to reject completely God's teachings concerning His new
creation.

12

An Unbroken Chain

FOR WHOM He did foreknow, He also did predestinate to be conformed to the image of His Son. . . . Moreover whom He did predestinate, them He also called: and whom He called, them He also justified: and whom He justified, them He also glorified" (Rom. 8:29, 30).

This is an unbroken chain of things that God *has done* for the saved one. All is based on His foreknowledge and culminates in glorification. *All is in the past tense, therefore already accomplished.*

The words "whom" and "them" are in each case coextensive. There is no stage at which there is the slightest possibility that the number of individuals is reduced. *Just as many are glorified as are predestinated. Not a single one less!* As all who are called are glorified, not one can be lost.

There are five doctrines of the Grace of God in this passage. Not a single one of them can be fully accepted without accepting the doctrine of eternal security of the believer.

1. GOD FOREKNOWS

The foreknowledge of God is a part of His omniscience. To say that God is omniscient is to say

67

that He knows everything—past, present and future. This He declares of Himself: "I am God, and there is none like Me, declaring the end from the beginning and from ancient times the things that are not yet done" (Isa. 46:9, 10).

In the following passages the foreknowledge of God is made the very basis for salvation. "For whom He did foreknow, He also did predestinate to be conformed to the image of His Son" (Rom. 8:29).

"According as He hath chosen us in Him before the foundation of the world, that we should be holy and without blame before Him in love" (Eph. 1:4).

"Elect according to the foreknowledge of God the Father" (1 Pet. 1:2).

These passages state clearly that what God has done in salvation was based on His foreknowledge. *He knew before Adam was created, or before a single saved person was saved, every detail of each life from the cradle to the grave. In view of this foreknowledge, He "predestinated" and He "chose." If it is possible by sin in the life, or by loss of faith, or by "willing to go away from God" to be lost, what can be said about the foreknowledge of God? If God did not see these things He is not omniscient. If He saw them and in spite of them undertook to predestinate, to call, to justify, and glorify, He started something which He cannot finish.*

Only by accepting the doctrine of the eternal security of the believer can one accept without reservation the doctrine of the omniscience of God.

2. HE ALSO DID PREDESTINATE

Predestination, as defined by Dr. Scofield, is "that effective exercise of the will of God by which things before determined by Him are brought to pass."

In this discussion, predestination is considered only with reference to the saved. These are said to be predestinated to be conformed to the image of God's Son. (See also Eph. 1:5, 1 Cor. 15:49, 1 John 3:2.)

God, therefore, by the effective exercise of His will has determined that all who are saved shall be conformed to the image of Christ.

If a single saved person is lost, God has failed as far as such an one is concerned to exercise His will effectively, and has not accomplished that which He determined to do. *To say that one who has been saved can be lost is to deny that God has power to do what He has determined to do.* One must either accept at full value God's own statement, or else reject it. There is no middle ground. One cannot even admit the "possibility" of a saved person being lost.

To emphasize the certainty of predestination, it is said to be "according to the good pleasure of His will" (Eph. 1:5). How then dare anyone say that a man can *will to go away from God* and be lost? That would clearly be interference with the pleasure of God's will and is a direct denial of God's own Word.

When God clearly says that He shall conform those who are saved into the image of His own Son, there is only one thing to do. That is to believe it. Any other attitude rejects this great doctrine.

3. HE ALSO CALLED

The calling of God is unto "the obtaining of the glory of our Lord Jesus Christ" (2 Thess. 2:14). It is according to His *own purpose* and does not depend, at any time, upon the saved one's own works. For it is written: "Who hath saved us, and called us with an holy calling, not according to our works, but according to His own purpose and grace, which was given us in Christ Jesus before the world began" (2 Tim. 1:9).

This purpose of God in calling is to make known the riches of His glory, through those called, who are "vessels of mercy which He had afore prepared unto glory" (Rom. 9:23, 24). "Unto them which are called, Christ the power of God" (1 Cor. 1:24). The faithfulness of God is involved in the calling (1 Cor. 1:9). Again, the calling shall not be altered. Israel was nationally broken off as the branches of the olive tree, but shall be grafted in again, "for all Israel shall be saved." This is because "the gifts and calling of God are without repentance" (Rom. 11:29).

The calling of God then is the carrying out of His own purpose, independent of the saved one's works. It is to make known the riches of His glory through the vessels of mercy. Christ (not they themselves) is the power of all that are called. The calling is based upon God's faithfulness and is without repentance.

All who are saved are called (2 Tim. 1:9).

Therefore, in order that one who has been saved, be lost, God must, by something in the life of such an one, be thwarted in His purpose. He will fail to make known the riches of His glory through that vessel of mercy. Christ is an insufficient power in that individual; God is not faithful, and He does repent. To say that one who has been saved is not eternally secure is to bring these charges against God.

4. HE ALSO JUSTIFIED

Justification is that act of God by which He imputes (or counts) righteousness to one who believes in Jesus Christ as the One Who was "made sin for us . . . that we might be made the righteousness of God in Him" (2 Cor. 5:21). It is entirely apart from any merit on the part of man, so that boasting might be excluded (Rom. 3:27).

Justification is through the redemption that is in Christ Jesus (Rom. 3:24). Because Christ was set forth as a propitiation for sin, God is able to justify the one that believes in Jesus and still remain just (Rom. 3:25, 26).

It is not a process that is being perfected as long as the believer continues to believe, but is a single act of God performed the instant an individual exercises faith in Jesus Christ. It is repeatedly spoken of as finished. (Rom. 5:21, 8:30, 1 Cor. 6:11, Tit. 3:7).

It is also an unalterable condition of every saved person. The righteousness that is imputed in justi-

fication is a free gift (Rom. 3:24; 5:17). As God
never repents the giving of His gifts (Rom. 11:29),
He will never count one who has been justified as
anything else than righteous.

Justification is by grace (Rom. 3:24). Therefore,
it is certain. That which is by grace is unfailing.
". . . it is of faith, that it might be by grace; to the
end that the promise might be sure to all the seed"
(Rom. 4:16).

All who are saved are justified. In order for one
who has been saved to be lost, he must lose his
standing before God as justified. To do so, some deficiency in the redemption of Christ and His death
as a propitiation must be found, for justification is
based entirely on that, apart from any merit or demerit of man. If a person can throw away his salvation as some say, it would be necessary for such an
one to have access to God's accounting records and
change them, for imputation of righteousness is a
matter of God's reckoning. It would be necessary for
God to take back a gift, which He never does. The
promise according to Grace which God says is sure
would have to fail.

5. ALREADY GLORIFIED

Those who hold that one who has been saved can
be lost will unhesitatingly agree that when the saints
reach glory there is no more danger of being lost.
These friends overlook the fact that *believers are already glorified* and that *it is but the manifestation of
the reality that is still in the future.* There are things

which God has already accomplished, but the manifestation thereof has been delayed until later. Thus, Christ is said to be the "Lamb foreordained before the foundation of the world, but manifest in these last times" (1 Pet. 1:20).

Similarly, the believer is already glorified. "Whom He justified, them He also glorified." But the manifestation thereof is in the future. "Your life is hid with Christ in God. When Christ, Who is our life, shall appear, then shall we also appear with Him in glory" (Col. 3:3, 4). *The glorification has taken place, though appearance in glory is in the future and in the meantime the believer's life is "hid with Christ in God." Can anyone be more secure?*

If one who is saved can be lost, it must have to be by taking such an one from his place in glory where he is *hid in God.* Certainly no one dares to say that this is possible. There are those who enthusiastically preach that the believer's inheritance is secure, because it is reserved in heaven. Yet they strongly deny the security of the believer. Have they overlooked the fact that the believer is already glorified, and that his life is not only in heaven but in God? It is impossible to accept the truth that the believer is already glorified and deny his eternal security.

"What shall we then say to these things? If God be for us, who can be against us? He that spared not His own Son, but delivered Him up for us all, how shall He not with Him also freely give us all things?" (Rom. 8:31, 32).

13

God's Judgments of the Sins of the Saved

G OD CANNOT ignore the sins of the unsaved. They must be judged. Neither can He ignore even the so-called smallest sin of one who is saved. Many who oppose the doctrine of the security of the believer freely consent to and teach, that God is merciful and will overlook the faults of those who are saved. This is error of the grossest kind. It means nothing less than that God compromises His own righteousness. Then He would not be God.

God always judges sin in the life of a believer. In fact He has made a twofold provision for judging such sin!

This judgment is twofold in that it is penal and corrective. The purpose of the penal judgment is to satisfy fully the demands of His righteousness. The corrective judgment is to satisfy His everlasting love (Jer. 31:3). Thus neither His righteousness nor His love is compromised.

This dual judgment of the sins of the saved is seen in the advocacy of Christ and in the chastening by the Father. *If it can be shown that God has made provision to keep the saved one from being lost, when he may commit sin after he has been saved, then the case is settled; for every cause that has ever*

74

been offered as a condition by which one may be lost, is in fact sin. It is sometimes admitted that one who has been saved might sin, and still not be lost; but it is said that if he stops believing, he is lost. That is just one form of sin, for "whatsoever is not of faith is sin" (Rom. 14:23). Again it is said that one can, of his own will, go away from God and be lost. Again, this is sin, for the setting up of one's will against the will of God is sin in its very essence. There is but one problem and that is SIN.

THE ADVOCACY OF CHRIST

"My little children, these things write I unto you, that ye sin not. And if any man sin, we have an Advocate with the Father, Jesus Christ the Righteous: and He is the propitiation for our sins: and not for ours only, but also for the sins of the whole world" (1 John 2:1, 2).

The scene here is on legal ground. Sin, the violation of God's holy law, is being judged. The sinner has an Advocate Who is righteous in the sight of the law. The Advocate is pleading the case on the basis of a propitiation. Propitiation means that the penalty has been paid. An advocate always pleads before a judge. The Judge is He Who is the Judge of the whole world. But He is also called "the Father." Therefore it is a son that is being judged. There must also be an accuser to bring the charge. Elsewhere (Rev. 12:10) it is revealed that he is Satan.

Satan is before God day and night accusing the brethren. When a saved person sins, Satan files a

prompt charge and demands condemnation, i. e.,
the full penalty of the law. He himself is under that
same penalty because iniquity was found in his
heart (Ezek. 28:15, 16). In the face of this accusa-
tion what is the hope of the sinning "saved one"?
God cannot overlook that sin. He would compromise His own righteousness by ignoring the sin
of the sinning "brother" and holding Satan responsible for his sin.

There is indeed need of an advocate! What plea
has the sinning saint to offer? And do not forget that
all who have been saved are in this position at some
time or other—some oftener, some less often. "If we
say that we have not sinned, we make Him a liar,
and His Word is not in us" (1 John 1:10).

*Thank God! There is an Advocate. He is the only
hope of the believer. It all depends on Him.* He is
Jesus Christ the *Righteous.* Being righteous, He has
never broken God's holy law. He is perfect in its
sight. Furthermore, He cannot do anything that will
compromise that law. Therefore, His advocacy is a
righteous one, and is in harmony with the law.

What then does He plead on behalf of the sinning
saint? It is the fact that He is the propitiation for
sins. He points to that hill outside of Jerusalem
where there were three crosses. On two, hung men
who were paying the penalty for their sins against
human laws. On the center one, was hanging One,
Who was the Son of man, yea also the Son of God.
He was there paying the penalty for sins of others.
He was there as the "Lamb of God Who taketh away

the sin of the world" (John 1:29). It is He Himself
that He points to and, as the Advocate of the sinning
saint, He pleads: "I am that Lamb without blemish
and spot (1 Pet. 1:19). I am that just One dying for
the unjust (1 Pet. 3:18). I was bruised for his iniq-
uities (Isa. 53:5). I bore his sins in My body upon
that tree (1 Pet. 2:24). I have redeemed him from
the curse of this law under which he is now being
accused, because I was made a curse for him (Gal.
3:13). I, the Righteous, was there made sin for him,
that he might be made righteous in the sight of this
holy law (2 Cor. 5:21)."

That is a picture of the Advocate, and that is, in
God's own words, the ground for His pleading. On
the basis of that' plea both the holy law and the
righteousness of the Judge are held inviolate.

Paul had grasped the full glory and significance of
this when he, through inspiration exclaimed: "Who
shall lay anything to the charge of God's elect? It is
God that justifieth. Who is he that condemneth? It
is Christ that died, yea rather, that is risen again,
Who is even at the right hand of God, Who also
maketh intercession for us" (Rom. 8:33, 34).

And then in the light of full satisfaction, both past
and present, of God's righteousness, he further ex-
claims: "Who shall separate us from the love of
God?" And his answer, so full of assurance (vv.
35-39) can be summed up in the one word—
NOTHING.

The tremendous significance of this present work
of Christ can be somewhat understood from the

comparison that is made of it with His own redemptive work.

"Much more then, being now justified by His blood, we shall be saved from wrath through Him, for if, when we were yet sinners, we were reconciled to God by the death of His Son, much more, being reconciled, we shall be saved by His life" (Rom. 5:9, 10).

Is the saved one now justified? Unquestionably. *"Much more"* then . . . *he shall be saved from wrath;* i. e., from the penalty of God's holy law. God's "shall" is certainty, but this is a "much more" shall. *The saved person can be much more certain of salvation from wrath than he can be of the already certain fact of justification! This is to the extent that life is much more than death. Reconciliation,—salvation of the past—is by His death. Salvation of the present and the future is by His resurrection life.* How dare finite mind question such a declaration by God? Can the finite understand the infinite? No. But with simple God-given faith man can say, "I believe."

And still God's revelation of this unsearchable theme is not exhausted. It has pleased Him to reveal clearly that *there is to be no interruption to this advocacy.* "But this Man, because He continueth ever, hath an unchangeable priesthood. Wherefore He is able also to save them to the uttermost that come unto God by Him, seeing He ever liveth to make intercession for them" (Heb. 7:24, 25).

The altogether too common interpretation of the

words, "save to the uttermost," is that God can take a sinner, even when sunk in the lowest depths of sin, and raise him to glory. Undoubtedly this has helped many who have seen themselves so low in sin that they have considered themselves as hopeless. Yet this is not what God intends. Such an interpretation permits degrees of sin more or less difficult for God to deal with. Scripture does not support this idea. *Twice in the two verses, the ever existent nature of the Intercessor is made the condition for His ability to save to the uttermost.* Furthermore, the words of the original here translated "to the uttermost" are in John 13:1, translated "unto the end." Therefore *the essential revelation in this passage is that the salvation, which is accomplished by the resurrection life of Christ, is without interruption.* It is an *eternal salvation* (Heb. 5:9).

The advocacy of Christ is therefore a provision to guarantee the eternal security of every believer.

GOD'S CHASTENING

God's provision in Christ's advocacy on behalf of the saved one is not all that He does for the specific purpose of keeping him from condemnation. There is a corrective judgment provided for sin which is not self-judged. This judgment of sin is chastening.

"To chasten is to purify morally and spiritually by the providential visitation of distress and affliction; to purify from errors or faults as the effect of discipline. It implies imperfection, but not guilt."

This is exactly what God does with the Christian

who fails to judge himself. One purpose of God's chastening is that the one chastened shall not be "condemned with the world." In other words, *this chastening is for the purpose of keeping the saved one from becoming lost.* "For if we would judge ourselves, we should not be judged. But when we are judged, we are chastened of the Lord, that we should not be condemned with the world" (1 Cor. 11:31, 32).

Chastening is a provision of God exclusively for those who are sons; that is, saved. *It is for no others and no son is excluded* (Heb. 12:6-8).

If God has made a special provision for the saved person who persists in sinning, to keep him from being lost, how can he be lost? It is a case of denying the sufficiency of God's provision in chastening to say that one who has been saved is not eternally secure.

The same provision is found in the Old Testament and is stated in unmistakeable words. It is a part of God's unconditional covenant with David.

"I will set up thy seed after thee, . . . and I will establish his kingdom . . . and I will establish the throne of his kingdom for ever. . . . I will be his Father, and he shall be My son. *If he commit iniquity, I will chasten him with the rod of men, and with the stripes of the children of men: but My mercy shall not depart away from him,* as I took it from Saul, whom I put away before thee" (2 Sam. 7:12-15).

Notice that God says very definitely that even

though iniquity (which is sin) is committed, His "mercy shall not depart." As long as God deals in mercy it is impossible to be lost.

Someone may argue that as God took His mercy from Saul so will He take it from the saved one who sins. In the first place, this would deny God's statement that He chastens the saved one in order that he be not condemned with the world. In the second place, the case of Saul and the saved person is not the same. Corrective chastening was not a part of the mercy that God showed to Saul and that He took away from him. It is very definitely a part of God's mercy toward the saved one as it was to David's son. The unsaved are objects of God's mercy, but there is no corrective chastening in that mercy and it shall be taken from them if they do not become saved.

But how did God dare to say that sin on the part of David's seed would not result in his rejection? There are present-day preachers who criticize similar statements to God's children of this age. If God Himself exalts His grace as being greater than the sins of one of His children, how dare any one condemn the one who similarly glorifies God's grace in this age? It is a serious matter to criticize the exaltation of the grace of God. This is the very purpose of salvation. It is "to the praise of the glory of His grace" (Eph. 1:6).

The one who fights the doctrine of security of the believer, as some are now doing, says that God will take His grace away from the sinning saint. Are they not then doing the very opposite to praising the glory of the grace of God? Is this not sin? If it is possible to become lost, what is their position? Are they not advocating their own condemnation?

Surely God has made ample provision by the advocacy of Christ to meet Satan's accusations and by chastening to correct the life of the saved one to keep him saved. Is it possible to accept at full value God's revelation of these provisions and still say that the believer is not eternally secure?

14

The Office of the Holy Spirit

THERE CAN be no adequate understanding of the purpose of the Holy Spirit's presence in the world as long as one rejects the doctrine of eternal security.

TO ABIDE FOREVER

Just before Jesus left this earth, He promised those that were His: "I will pray the Father, and He shall give you another Comforter, that He may abide with you forever . . . He dwelleth with you, and shall be in you" (John 14:16, 17).

Therefore, in this age the Holy Spirit dwells in the individual believer and is there to *abide forever.*

It is true that David prayed, "Cast me not away from Thy presence and take not Thy Holy Spirit from me" (Psa. 51:11). But that was before Jesus had prayed that the Holy Spirit should abide forever. That makes a vast difference. The Holy Spirit can be grieved (Eph. 4:30) and may be quenched (1 Thess. 5:19) so that His voice is not heard; but this does not imply that He is taken away.

The Holy Spirit never dwells in a lost person. Such an one is spiritually dead, which means that he is separated from the Spirit. It is a contradiction, then, of the promise which Jesus gave to His dis-

83

ciples, to say that one in whom the Holy Spirit has come to abide forever, can be lost.

SEALED, AS TO POSITION

Believers are sealed by the Holy Spirit unto the day of redemption (Eph. 4:30). What is the purpose of that sealing?

In Revelation (Chap. 7:2-8) is a company of servants of God who are sealed in their foreheads. The purpose of this seal was to keep them secure (Rev. 9:4).

After Daniel had been cast into the lion's den, "a stone was brought, and laid upon the mouth of the den; and the King sealed it with his own signet, and with the signet of his lords; that the purpose might not be changed concerning Daniel" (Dan. 6:17).

In his vision, John saw Satan bound for a thousand years, cast into the bottomless pit, and shut up; and a seal was set upon him that he should deceive the nations no more, till the thousand years should be fulfilled (Rev. 20:2, 3).

In the first case, the servants were sealed so as to be secure against the torments of the locusts. In the second case, the seal was applied so that there could be no change in the King's command. In the third instance, the seal assures that Satan will be in a place of safe keeping from which he cannot escape.

In all three instances, the seal denotes an unalterable position of those who are sealed. That is exactly what the Holy Spirit as a seal means to the saved person. God has sealed him by His own Spirit so that he, as a believer, cannot be changed until the day of redemption.

SEALED AS TO OWNERSHIP

The seal also signifies ownership. Everyone who believes is sealed with the Holy Spirit "until the redemption of the purchased possession" (Eph. 1:14). This sealing then is effective and cannot be broken as long as a believer is in this mortal body. It is not needed after that. Those whom Christ has purchased with His own blood shall always be His very own. As the seal cannot be broken, they are secure. (See also page 43.)

EARNEST OF INHERITANCE

In addition to all the above, the Holy Spirit is given as an earnest of the believer's inheritance (Eph. 1:14). Earnest money is a payment made by a purchaser to guarantee the completion of the transaction by him. In Christ, the believer has obtained an inheritance which was "predestinated according to the purpose of Him Who worketh all things after the counsel of His own will" (Eph. 1:11).

The believer has not as yet entered into possession of this inheritance, but the Holy Spirit has been given as an earnest that it shall be given when the transaction has been fully consummated. To say that one who has been saved can be lost is to say that possession of the inheritance shall not be given to one to whom God has already made an earnest payment. "God is not a man that He should lie; neither the son of man that He should repent: hath He said and shall He not do it? Or hath He spoken, and shall He not make it good?" (Num. 23:19).

Thus the doctrine of the eternal security of the believer is required by the fact that the Holy Spirit has come into the saved one to abide forever; he is sealed by the Holy Spirit, both for the purpose of security and as a sign of ownership due to purchase; and God has given Him as a pledge to the believer that he shall receive an inheritance in heaven.

If the believer is not eternally secure, what does all of this teaching concerning the Holy Spirit mean?

15

Objects of the Love of God

MAN MAY be either the object of the love of God or the wrath of God. There is no middle ground. Those who are lost are called the children of wrath (Eph. 2:3). In fact, being the object of wrath constitutes being lost (John 3:36). On the other hand to be saved is to be an object of His love. "Having loved His own, He loved them unto the end" (or, to the uttermost). (John 13:1).

If it be possible for one who has been saved to be lost, it must of necessity be possible for one who has been the object of the love of God to be taken out of that position and be made the object of the wrath of God. Does any Scripture passage teach that? Definitely, No. On the contrary, it is taught that God loves His own with an everlasting love (Jer. 31:3). All saints of this Age were chosen in Christ before the foundation of the world that they should be before Him in love throughout all eternity (Eph. 1:4).

This is a part of the purpose of God in order to bring praise to the glory of His grace (Eph. 1:5, 6). If it were possible to revert into the state of being a child of wrath, then God can be thwarted in His purpose. It has been pointed out elsewhere (see page 57) that that is not possible.

Furthermore God says, in the most emphatic and

87

comprehensive language, that nothing, or no one, can separate the believer from the love of God which is in Christ Jesus. "For I am persuaded, that neither death, nor life, nor angels, nor principalities, nor powers, nor things present, nor things to come, nor height, nor depth, nor any other creature, shall be able to separate us from the love of God which is in Christ Jesus our Lord" (Rom. 8:38, 39).

Even so, there are those who make all this void by saying, "While it is true that nothing can separate a believer from the love of God, he can of his own will, go away from God's love." This statement is due to a false understanding of the free agency of man (see page 117). The passage itself here in Romans eight also clearly excludes any such possibility.

Several "creatures" are mentioned as being unable to "separate us from the love of God." Then in order to leave no possible chance for doubt, these words are added, "nor any other creature." As every believer is a creature of God, he is also included in the words "any other creature." It is, therefore, a flat denial of God's Word to say that a man can separate himself from God's love. *If anything is emphatically taught in the Bible, it is that when man has become the object of the everlasting love of God, there is no change in that condition.*

God so loved the world that He gave His only begotten Son to satisfy the demands of His own righteousness. Those who reject that Son are under the wrath of God, but whosoever accepts that Son as the One upon Whom the wrath of God was poured because of his sin, he is then and thereby unalterably made the object of the everlasting love of God. It is every believer's privilege to rejoice in this glorious revelation of God's love. To deny the eternal security of the believer is to rob many of this rejoicing.

THE SOVEREIGN GRACE OF GOD

One who is the object of the love of God is under the sovereign grace of God. The unsaved man is under the condemnation of the law. Sin reigns in his life unto death (Rom. 5:21).

That which is sovereign is independent of, and unlimited by any other. It is supreme or highest power. Therefore, where sin reigns, grace cannot be sovereign and where grace is sovereign, sin has no dominion.

When grace has become sovereign, sin can never again reign, for it is said: "Sin shall not have dominion over you: for ye . . . are under grace" (Rom. 6:14). Notice that it is *shall not* (not *does not*) which indicates that *the reign of sin unto death has been definitely brought to an end.* Thus the grace of God is the supreme power and reigns unto eternal life in the case of everyone that comes under its sovereignty.

That the grace of God is sovereign can mean nothing less than that the believer is eternally secure. If one who has been saved could be lost because of sin (and remember that is the only thing that can cause anyone to be lost) then sin would have to become a greater power than grace which is impossible.

In the covenant made with David (previously referred to), God specifically said that even if David's son would commit iniquity, His mercy would not depart away from him (2 Sam. 7:14, 15). This shows that sin in the life of one in a covenant relationship to God, does not limit the sovereignty of His grace.

To deny the eternal security of the believer is to deny the sovereignty of the grace of God. One who does not see himself eternally secure under the sovereign grace of God can never sing with the psalmist: "O give thanks unto the Lord: for He is good: for His mercy endureth for ever" and under all circumstances of life, repeat that refrain twenty-five times (Psa. 136).

16

Kept by the Power of God

JESUS PRAYED: "Holy Father, keep through Thine own Name those whom Thou hast given Me, that they may be one, as We are" (John 17:11). Peter who heard that prayer wrote some years later: "Kept by the power of God through faith unto salvation ready to be revealed in the last time" (1 Pet. 1:5).

A. IS GOD OMNIPOTENT?

Thus those who are saved have been committed by Jesus, Who for them gave His Own life, to God for safe keeping. *If God fails to keep a single one of those whom Christ bought with His own blood, He fails to conserve that which was accomplished by the death and resurrection of Christ.* God forbid the thought.

There is a need today that believers know that they are being kept by the power of God. Paul realized this in his day, and wrote to the Ephesian saints, to "the faithful in Christ Jesus," that he prayed that they might know "what is the exceeding greatness of His power to us-ward who believe." Then he described that power as: "His mighty power, which He wrought in Christ, when He raised Him from the dead and set Him at His own right

91

hand in the heavenly places, far above all principality, and power, and might, and dominion, and every name that is named, not only in this world but also in that which is to come; and hath put all things under His feet and gave Him to be the head over all things to the Church" (Eph. 1:19-22).

No finite mind can fathom the "exceeding greatness" of this power, but everyone who believes may know in simple faith that this power is exercised in his behalf.

This power of God, in raising Christ from the dead, transcends every other power, for it raised Christ from a death which was caused by the sum total of human sin and placed Him far above every other power that is named in this world and in that to come. It is nothing less than omnipotence.

As this power was greater than all human sin, it is surely greater than the sins of any single saved person. As it is clearly stated that this power is exercised on behalf of everyone that believes, it is nothing less than a denial of the omnipotence of God to say that by sinning, or by ceasing to believe, or by willing to go away from God, a saved person can be lost.

As this power is the greatest expression concerning God's power, it can be said, to use the words of another, "the universe will crumble before a single saved one can be lost."

To deny the eternal security of the believer is to deny the omnipotence of God.

B. WAS CHRIST RAISED FROM THE DEAD?

The resurrection of Christ is considered in God's Word as guaranteeing the resurrection of believers. Both are by the same power. "God hath both raised up the Lord, and will also raise up us by His own power" (1 Cor. 6:14).

Jesus Himself gave the fact of His resurrection as a guarantee of the resurrection of believers. He said, "Because I live, ye shall live also" (John 14:19). The same truth is also found in Romans 8:11. "But if the Spirit of Him that raised up Jesus from the dead dwell in you, He that raised up Christ from the dead shall also quicken your mortal bodies by His Spirit that dwelleth in you."

One who is lost has no part in the resurrection of the saints. But God's Word to those who are saved is, that they shall have part in that resurrection and points to the resurrection of Christ as evidence of that fact. Thus the denial of the security of the believer questions the power of God to raise up those that are saved. It implies that something might happen in the life of a saved one to interfere with the operation of God's power. And if this is possible, then is there not also room even to question the resurrection of Christ as having taken place?

Thus it is seen that the denial of the security of the believer raises questions as to the power of God and as to the resurrection of Christ, the very ground for the hope of eternal life.

17

Some Pertinent Questions

MUCH MORE could have been written than space here permits; but from the foregoing, it is clear that the doctrines of the grace of God demand the doctrine of eternal security, and that the doctrines of grace are made void by the contention that one who has been saved can be lost.

Those who deny the eternal security of the believer and teach that one who has been saved can be lost, must show how that can happen in view of all that has been said. They must answer the following questions:

How can one, who has received Christ and all things with Him as a gift which God says He does not repent of, be lost when the possession of this gift means eternal life?

How can one whose salvation does not depend in the slightest upon human effort or merit, but entirely upon the power of God and the merits of Christ, be lost by some human act, either by the mind or by the body?

How can one for whom Christ by His death paid the full penalty of the law, and satisfied all the demands of God's justice, be made to pay that penalty again?

How can one who has been redeemed by an eternal redemption and by the precious blood of Christ, which has infinite value, be returned to a state of condemnation?

How can one who has been born of incorruptible (undying) seed and thus given eternal life as a gift of which God does not repent, die?

How can one whom God says shall not come into condemnation, come into condemnation?

How can one who is a new creature and in a new creation in which sin, condemnation and death are not known and in which the unalterable law is life, ever be condemned and die?

If *every believer* was foreknown of God, and *all* who were foreknown were predestinated to become conformed to the image of the Son of God, and *all* who were predestinated have been called, and *all* who were called have been justified, and *all* who were justified have already been glorified in the sight of God, at what point is it possible for a single one to be lost?

If God has made provision for every saved person through the advocacy of Christ, which is based solely on His righteousness and the fact that His death was a propitiation for *all* sin, to answer all charges made by the accuser against him, how can such an one be condemned (lost)?

If in every saved person the Holy Spirit abides forever; if he is sealed with the Holy Spirit for security and sealed and witnessed as to Christ's ownership; and if he has been given the Spirit as a guarantee of something which he can only receive when he reaches glory, how can he be anything but eternally secure?

If being an object of God's wrath is to be lost and being an object of His love is to be saved, and if God says that one who has become an object of His love shall always be so; in fact that is the very purpose of salvation: how can one be lost?

If God declares that He is exercising the very same power on behalf of the saved one as He did when He raised Christ from the dead and set Him at the greatest height of power and glory, how can it be said that is is possible for one who has been saved to be cast by God into the lake of fire which means being lost?

It seems then, that those who deny the eternal security of the believers must honestly face every one of these questions and prove by Scripture passages that their position does not contradict, but harmonizes with all of the doctrines of the grace of God. Until they do this, they are unquestionably subject to the charge that they are teaching against the grace of God.

Until that has been done, the eternal security of every believer will stand as the most strongly attested revelation in God's Word.

18

Grace Teaches—Love Constrains

IN PART II, it was shown that the doctrines of the grace of God cannot be understood and fully accepted without the acceptance of the truth of eterna. security. This section deals similarly with eternal security in its relation to godly living, or practical Christianity.

The great and widely accepted charge against the teaching of eternal security is that it leads to carelessness in the lives of Christians and robs the Church of its spiritual power. It is said that to teach that one who has been saved cannot be lost is to offer a license to sin. Incidents from the lives of individuals are cited as proof of this contention. The *argument is always founded upon human observations and judgments.*

In reply, much evidence might be offered both from the lives of living Christians and from history to refute this charge. The lives of the Puritans, who held this truth, are outstanding illustrations which might be used with considerable effect. But *in a discussion of an issue as infinite as this is, finite observations and often fallible conclusions based upon them, cannot be considered as conclusive evidence. The only evidence that can be admitted as final is that which is taken from God's own revelation, the Bible. That is absolute and infallible.* Those who make the charge that teaching eternal security is to offer a license to sin never support their charge with any Scripture passage.

The fact is, the charge that teaching eternal security leads to carelessness in Christian living is a direct contradiction of God's Word. *Many of the strongest appeals in the Bible for a pure, holy, righteous and godly life are based on statements which definitely teach the eternal security of the believer.* This being true, as will be shown extensively in the following chapters, it is those who deny the eternal security of the believer and thereby rob these passages of their true and full meaning who are contributing to the low state of standards of Christian living. This can hardly be overstated.

God does not, as is the popular conception, make righteous living the condition for eternal life and glory with Him. That, as has already been shown, is a matter of pure grace. *It is the fact of eternal life and assurance of glory and all that these include that is the incentive to holy living. It is what God has already done through the operation of His Sovereign grace.* It is the doctrines of the grace of God which have been shown to demand the doctrine of eternal security upon which God rests His appeal for practical righteousness. Men who teach against eternal security do not fully understand these doctrines and therefore cannot appeal to holiness on God's own basis.

It is not God's holiness nor His righteousness; it is not the law, nor is it the threat of condemnation (being lost) that teaches Christians to live soberly, righteously and godly. *It is His grace that does so.* Paul wrote to Titus giving instructions as to what he should teach as rules of conduct. Then he gave the reason for so writing in these words: "For the grace of God that bringeth salvation hath appeared to all men, teaching us that, denying ungodliness and worldly lusts, we should live soberly, righteously and godly in this present world" (Tit. 2:11, 12).

Thus, those who limit the grace of God by denying the eternal security of the believer, limit that which God says teaches godly living; while those who magnify His grace are teaching that which God says teaches believers how to live well pleasing unto Him.

It is important to be guided, not by what man's judgments or conclusions teach, but by that which God's Word reveals.

THE LOVE OF CHRIST CONSTRAINS US

As the grace of God teaches how to live as chil dren of God ought to live, so it is the love of Christ that constrains or compels the saved one so to live. Paul says "For the love of Christ constraineth us" (2 Cor. 5:14). Therefore, fear of the wrath of God (being lost) cannot be the dynamic of holy and righteous living. Neither can it be said that it is the righteousness or holiness of God that is the constraining influence.

It is that love that was expressed when Christ died and rose again. It was through that death and resurrection that all old things passed away, yea even the curse and condemnation of the law, and the believer became a new creature in Christ that cannot die (see Chapter XI). It is that love of God which He manifested when He was in Christ on the cross, reconciling the world unto Himself (2 Cor. 5:-15-19). It is that love of God from which the believer cannot be separated (see Chapter XV), and which guarantees the eternal security of everyone that has become the object thereof.

If Paul's statement is true, then to proclaim that love, to magnify it, to call attention to its eternal and unchanging nature is to open the hearts and lives of Christians for that which constrains them to be what God would have them be. On the other hand, to deny the unbroken flow of this love, by saying that one who has been the object of it can be lost, is to hinder God's own dynamic from operating in the life of the saved one.

This is undoubtedly the greatest charge that can be brought against the teaching that those whom God through infinite love, expressed in the death of His Son, has saved, can be lost.

It is grace that teaches and the love of Christ that constrains believers to live as God would have them live. The need of the Church today is a clear teaching of this.

19

Incentives to a Surrendered Life

POSSIBLY THE strongest appeal to a life entirely surrendered to God is in the following words:
"I beseech you therefore, brethren, by the mercies of God, that ye present your bodies a living sacrifice, holy, acceptable unto God, which is your reasonable service. And be not conformed to this world: but be ye transformed by the renewing of your mind, that ye may prove what is that good, and acceptable and perfect will of God" (Rom. 12:1, 2).

Here is a plea to the believer that his body be made a living sacrifice. The word sacrifice signifies change of ownership for the purpose of being consumed for the benefit of the new owner. It includes a complete surrender of selfwill. This sacrifice is to be living, that is, continuous and productive of results. It is to be holy. It is to be acceptable to God. Furthermore, all conformity to this world is to end and the life shall be transformed through the mind's seeking the good and acceptable and perfect will of God. In this there is nothing left of self.

Paul does not make this strong appeal for a surrendered life without first stating very clearly and definitely the motive or incentive that prompts that kind of life. He does so in these words, *"I beseech you therefore, by the mercies of God."* The word "therefore" shows that he rests the whole argument on what he has in the preceding part of his letter taught about the mercies of God. These are the doctrines of the grace of God. This is always God's method. How different this is from the purely human and altogether unscriptural method of scolding and threatening Christians and using the element of fear that they may be lost, to arouse from worldly interests and to quicken interest in spiritual things!

As Paul pleads on the basis of the "mercies of God," it is perfectly clear that his appeal is without force until these mercies are known, understood and accepted. The better known and the more clearly understood these are, the greater is the force of the argument. On the other hand if these mercies of God are denied, then the force of the appeal is lost and there is no reason for heeding it.

Any appeal that is based on certain facts or conditions has force only in the same measure as is the certainty of those facts or conditions on which it is made. For years banks appealed to the public to make deposits because of the securities guaranteeing the repayment of the money. This appeal had force, and men, women and children, rich and poor, brought their savings. Why? Because the security of their funds was not questioned. But times changed. The banks' investments dropped in value. People began to question the security of their funds. Deposits dropped off. Withdrawals became greater and greater. The banks' appeals for deposits were without force because their argument based on safety was not accepted.

So it is in Christian life. God makes His appeals to the saved to invest their lives, their all with Him and offers His mercies as security. These mercies of God which He offers as securities are guaranteed by the precious blood of Christ. Are they certain? As long as His blood is efficacious, these securities are good. *Thus it is highly important both to know what the doctrines of the grace of God are and to understand them. They are seldom taught and, as much of the meaning of these doctrines is lost by the denial of the eternal security of the believer, it is not strange that Christians these days do not sacrifice their bodies to God as they ought to do.*

The all important thing then is to consider the "mercies of God" or the doctrines of the grace of God as set forth in that part of the letter to the Romans which precedes the appeal.

The first part of Romans (Rom. 1:18-3:20) deals with the sinfulness of man and concludes that there is none righteous and that the whole world is guilty before God. Man is shown to be incapable of doing anything towards his own justification. This is a prerequisite for the operation of the grace of God.

Against this background of utter helplessness and absolute hopelessness on man's part, the mercies of God are set forth.

But there is a righteousness for man. It is not by doing what the law commands. It is of God and is revealed in the Gospel (Rom. 1:17). It is manifested in the life of faith that Jesus Christ lived, and is unto and upon all that believe (Rom. 3:22). It is a gift from God (Rom. 5:17). Being a gift from God, this righteousness shall always be the posses-sion of him who has received it through faith, as has already been shown (p. 34).

The one unto whom this righteousness has been counted is said to be justified by grace (Rom. 4:24, 25). Inasmuch as justification is by grace, it is un-alterable (see p. 59). Justification is made possible by the redemption that is in Christ Jesus (Rom. 3:24). This again proves that it is unalterable, for redemption is eternal (see p. 42).

Those who have been justified henceforth stand in grace (Rom. 5:2). They are no longer under the law but are under grace (Rom. 6:14). One who is not under the law, which is the ministration (and only such) of condemnation, cannot be lost. There is no condemnation for them because they are in Christ Jesus. "There is therefore now no condemna-tion to them that are in Christ Jesus" (Rom. 8:1). If you are in Christ Jesus at this moment, you can-not be condemned and lost.

Another of God's mercies is the provision that those who have been justified shall be saved from wrath. This is "much more" sure than the fact that Christ died for them while sinners (Rom. 5:8, 9). This is accomplished by the present life of Christ (v. 10).

"As sin hath reigned unto death even so grace reigns unto eternal life" (Rom. 5:21). Therefore the one that is under grace is assured of eternal life. This eternal life is also said to be a "gift of God through Jesus Christ our Lord" (Rom. 6:23), and therefore always remains in the possession of the one who has received it.

The bodies of *all* in whom the Spirit dwells (and that includes all who have been saved) shall be quickened, that is raised up, by the Spirit of God that dwells in them (Rom. 8:11).

Believers have been predestinated to be conformed to the image of His Son. They are already glorified (vv. 29, 30). No one can condemn them, because Christ has died for them, yea rather, He is interceding for them (v. 34). Finally in the strongest language possible it is said to be impossible to become separated from the love of God (vv. 35-39).

These are the mercies of God upon which Paul rests his argument for a completely surrendered life in God's service. *Every one of these mercies is absolutely unalterable. The security that God offers His children when He pleads with them to invest their lives with Him cannot lose its value.* That is why the full surrender of self is a reasonable service.

Those who deny eternal security discount the value of every one of God's mercies and deny the efficacy of the shed blood of Christ. To them these have value only as long as the Christian does this or that, or keeps from doing this or that which they themselves specify. *Thus the whole appeal is lost, for the things added cause an appalling amount of uncertainty and confusion.* In view of this, who is it that is responsible for the lack of sacrificial Christian lives in the churches?

20

Walk Worthy of Calling

"I THEREFORE, THE prisoner in the Lord, beseech you to walk [live] worthily of the calling wherewith ye were called" (Eph. 4:1 R. V.). In the remaining part of this epistle, Paul discusses Christian conduct, all of which is part of living worthily of the calling, and therefore a part of the appeal. This appeal to those who have been saved by grace through faith to live a life worthy of their calling, is introduced by the word "therefore." Thus it becomes necessary to turn back and consider the reasons for the appeal. *No appeal to live worthily of one's station in life means anything without a knowledge of the importance of that position.*

In the first three chapters, the apostle has presented the believer's standing before God. It is these truths that are the basis for the appeal to walk worthily.

Believers have been chosen in Christ before the foundation of the world to be holy and without blame before God in love. They have been predestinated to be placed as sons. All of this has been done according to the good pleasure of the will of God and for the purpose of praise to the glory of His grace (Eph. 1:4-6). Choosing was according to His foreknowledge, so He made no mistake as to whom

He chose. As predestination is "that effective exercise of the will of God by which things before determined are brought to pass" (see p. 57), it is certain that nothing can interfere with the accomplishment of placing every believer as a son without blame before God in love. This is the same position that Christ had with the Father before the foundation of the world (John 17:24). It is the most exalted position into which any of God's creatures can ever be placed. It is above the whole of the heavenly host. As it is all of grace, and that which is of grace is certain (p. 25), there can be no question as to its accomplishment.

God has sealed with the Holy Spirit everyone that He has chosen. Repeated emphasis is placed on the fact that all that is done by God is "according to the purpose of Him Who worketh all things after the counsel of His own will" (see vv. 5, 9, 11). All of this is unto "the praise of the glory of His grace" (v. 6) and "unto the praise of His glory" (vv. 12, 14). There is no possibility of making any part of this conditional in the slightest upon human works or merit.

It is further revealed that God is exercising on behalf of the believer the same power that He exercised in that greatest manifestation of His power, when He raised Christ from the dead and set Him above all principality and power and might and dominion. If anything is certain, it must be that which is being accomplished by that power.

Salvation by grace through faith as a gift of God

apart from any work or merit of man, has already
been discussed (Chapter VI), and was shown to be
unalterable. This is a part of the high calling of God.

It is all of this and more too to which the word
"therefore" in Paul's appeal refers, and which is
made the basis for the appeal to live worthily of
God's calling.

Another appeal to walk worthy of God is found in
1 Thessalonians 2:11, 12. This is based on God's
calling the believer unto His Kingdom and glory.
As the calling of God is without repentance (Rom.
11:29) and is therefore unalterable, here again that
which assures the eternal security of the believer is
made the basis for the appeal.

This emphasis upon the certainty of the grounds
for these appeals must impress the careful Bible
student. To say that one who has been saved can be
lost is to inject an element of uncertainty into that
which God makes certain. It confuses that which
must be understood clearly to give force to the appeal, and thereby weakens the appeal. On the other
hand, *the teaching of eternal security honors and
illuminates every statement God makes concerning
those that are saved, so that the basis for the appeal
can be accepted, and the appeal understood.*

BE NOT CONFORMED TO THE WORLD

In order to walk worthy of God, it is necessary
that one be not conformed to the world, but separated from it. The apostle Paul also makes this ap-

peal and, as in the case of the appeal for full surrender of body and will and also the appeal to walk
worthy of God, this appeal also is based on conditions which guarantee the eternal security of the
believer.

In Romans 12:1, 2, previously considered, there
is an appeal to those who have received the mercies
of God that they be not conformed to the world.
Separation from the world is thus made directly
dependent upon the doctrines of the grace of God,
which, as was shown in the last preceding chapter,
demand the eternal security of the believer.

There are other passages in the doctrinal epistles
which are equally clear in dealing with this question
of separation from the world. Paul pleaded with the
Corinthian Christians to flee fornication and his appeal was based on the fact that their bodies were
members of Christ. This appeal was followed by an
appeal to glorify God in the body and in the spirit
because the body was the temple of the Holy Ghost
which was in them, and because they were bought
with a price (2 Cor. 6:15-20).

Here, then, two unalterable conditions are made
the basis for the appeal. The Holy Spirit Who was in
them was there to "abide forever" (John 14:16) and
the purchase by the blood of Christ had been both
sealed and witnessed by the Holy Spirit (see p. 44)
until the redemption of the body. *Thus again it is
the certainty and unchangeable work that God has
done for the believer that is the basis for the appeal.*

In 2 Corinthians 6:14-16 is an appeal to believers not to be unequally yoked with unbelievers, because they are the temple of the living God.

An appeal to set the affections on things above and not on things on the earth is based on one of the strongest statements in the Bible concerning the eternal security of the believer in these words: "Set your affection on things above, not on things on the earth, for ye are dead, and your life is hid with Christ in God" (Col. 3:2, 3). Can anyone be more secure than the one who has been hidden in God so that nothing can touch him?

This same appeal to nonconformity with the world because of what the believer is and because of God's purpose, is found in 1 Thessalonians 5:5, 6, 9, 10 (R. V.). "Ye are all sons of light and sons of the day: we are not of the night, nor of darkness, so then let us not sleep, as do the rest, but let us watch and be sober." "For God appointed us not unto wrath, but unto the obtaining of salvation through our Lord Jesus Christ, Who died for us, that, whether we wake or sleep, we should live together with Him."

Every one of the conditions upon which these various appeals are based is materially weakened, if not entirely destroyed, by the teaching that one who has been saved can be lost, for that denies the unalterable nature of these conditions.

It would seem, then, that worldliness in the church of today is chargeable to failure to teach the doctrines of the grace of God which are inseparable from the truth of eternal security. As denial of the truth of eternal security makes it impossible to teach these doctrines in their fullness, it follows that those who teach against that truth are contributing to the present state of worldliness in the churches.

21

An Appeal to Purity

AND EVERY man that hath this hope in him puri-fieth himself, even as He is pure" (1 John 3:3). This is an appeal to purity of life. The standard that is set is the perfect purity of Christ—nothing less than that. It is addressed to those who have a certain hope—to no others. What then is the hope? It is stated in the preceding verse. "Beloved, now are we the sons ['children' in the Revised Version] of God, and it doth not yet appear what we shall be: but we know that, when He shall appear, we shall be like Him; for we shall see Him as He is" (v. 2). This is an unqualified statement that those who are now children of God shall be like Christ. It is not, "those who remain children," or "remain faithful," or "hold out," it is all who are now children. And this "now" has been there during the entire Church age. This hope is "as an anchor of the soul, both sure and steadfast, and which entereth into that within the veil; whither the Forerunner is for us entered, even Jesus" (Heb. 6:19, 20).

It is because of this sure hope that those who have been saved are urged to purify themselves. A constant realization of the fact that one shall be like Jesus Christ, the Son of God, makes all filthiness of life seem strangely out of place.

But if a person has no definite assurance that he shall be like Him, then the appeal loses its force. *How many Christians are there not who do not K-N-O-W that they shall be like Christ! How can anyone know it if it is possible for him to be lost? If it is possible for any one saved person to be lost, that same possibility exists for all.* Thus none can know that they shall be like Christ if the teaching against eternal security is right. If no one can surely know that he shall be like Christ, then this appeal is just so many words wasted.

How different God's appeal is from that which is so often made from pulpits: "If you do not do this," or "if you do that," you will not be taken when Christ comes!

Thus the teaching of the eternal security of the believer supports God's appeal for purity of life while the denial thereof undermines it.

Another appeal to pure living is found in Colossians 3:5, 6 (R. V.). "Put to death therefore your members which are upon the earth: fornication, uncleanness, passion, evil desire, and covetousness, which is idolatry." Again the appeal is based on an unconditional statement to which the word "therefore" points back. It is this: "When Christ, Who is our life, shall be manifested, then shall ye also [who are hid with Him in God] be manifested with Him in glory." Again it is a definite, unconditional statement that connects the believer with Christ in glory that is the reason given as the incentive to purity. To teach that one who is saved might not appear with Christ in glory (that is, be lost) and that possibly because of one of the very sins enumerated, is to take away from such an one the incentive to purity that God has caused to be written down for his special help when he is about to sin.

DESIRE THE WORD OF GOD

God's appeal for purity of life is not merely negative; it is for the purpose of making the saved one desirous of the Word of God, as in the following appeal:

"Wherefore laying aside all malice, and all guile, and hypocrisies, and envies, and all evil speakings, as newborn babes, desire the sincere milk of the Word, that ye may grow thereby" (1 Pet. 2:1, 2). Here is an appeal which may well be heeded in many churches today. The things here mentioned are of a class that are usually not mentioned by those that oppose eternal security as causing one who has been saved to be lost. Such things as envies and evil speakings are so subtle and common that few Christians would escape being lost, if sin could cause a saved person to become lost. Yet Peter says lay all of these away and instead thereof desire the Word of God. What a need there is now to be occupied with the Word of God! Yes, and there is a crying need for the simple expository preaching of it.

This appeal is to persons who have been addressed as "elect according to the foreknowledge of God the Father" (1 Pet. 1:2). It has already been shown (p. 56) that election based on God's foreknowledge means eternal security or else God is not omniscient. Therefore in the very salutation these persons (and it is to all who are saved) are reminded of their eternal security in Christ.

But the appeal is based on a particular argument as is shown by the introductory word "wherefore." This argument is found in the last three verses of the previous chapter. "Being born again, not of corruptible seed, but of incorruptible, by the Word of God, which liveth and abideth for ever: For all flesh is as grass, and all the glory of man as the flower of grass. The grass withereth and the flower thereof falleth away: but the Word of the Lord endureth forever" (1 Pet. 1:23-25). The unending nature of that life which results from the new birth and which is offered as the sole argument for laying aside malice, envies, et cetera, and desiring the Word of God is the very heart of this passage. That life is not of corruptible, but of incorruptible seed.

This statement is both a negative and a positive statement. By the immutable law of birth, that which is born has the same nature as that which gave birth. The unending nature is asserted for the third time in the words "which liveth forever." Then the corruptible nature of flesh which is as grass, is contrasted with the new life which issues from the Word of God; and finally it is stated that the Word of God (which is the life of the saved one) endures forever. In no passage is the eternal nature of the new life of the saved one more forcefully stated. It is just this fact that is the reason given for those who are born again (saved) to lay aside malice and guile, and hypocrisies, and envies, and evil speakings and instead of these desire the Word of God.

If the fact of the unending nature of the new life of the saved one (which means that he is eternally secure) is denied, then there is very little left, if anything, upon which to appeal to saved people to lay aside all these things and to cultivate an appetite for God's Word. Nothing can more stimulate a desire for knowledge of God's Word than a clear understanding of the fact that one is born again of incorruptible seed and is certain of being in glory with Christ.

Thus again the appeal to a godly life is based on the security of the saved and a denial thereof robs the appeal of its force.

22

Steadfastness

IN 1 CORINTHIANS 15:58, Paul makes this most earnest plea: "My beloved brethren, be ye steadfast, unmovable, always abounding in the work of the Lord, forasmuch as ye know that your labour is not in vain in the Lord." Something has been said which gives assurance that their work shall not be in vain. What is this something? It is found in the preceding verses, going back as far as the fifty-first. "Behold I show you a mystery; We shall not all sleep, but we shall all be changed, in a moment, in the twinkling of an eye, at the last trump . . . For this corruptible must put on incorruption, and this mortal must put on immortality . . . then shall be brought to pass the saying that is written, Death is swallowed up in victory . . . But thanks be to God which giveth us the victory through our Lord Jesus Christ."

Those are the certain facts upon which the appeal to steadfastness, immovableness and a life abounding in the work of the Lord is made. Such work *cannot* be in vain because of the certainty of the facts upon which the appeal is based. What is it that is certain? *All* shall be changed. All who were members of "the church of God which is at Corinth," all who "are sanctified in Christ Jesus," all who are

117

"called to be saints, with all that in every place call upon the Name of Jesus Christ our Lord" (1 Cor. 1:2). These saints in Corinth did not have the best record, yet Paul made no exception. He stipulated no conditions nor is there any that can be implied. It is "we shall *all* be changed." This is so because the victory over death is by God through Jesus Christ, and "God is faithful, by Whom ye were called unto the fellowship of His Son Jesus Christ our Lord" (1 Cor. 1:9).

If it is possible for any one who is now saved to be excluded from that "all" and not be given the victory over death by Jesus Christ, the appeal loses its force. If there is any possibility that one now saved might not be "changed" at the last trump, then there is a chance that such an one has worked for the Lord in vain. If anyone who is saved can be lost, then whatever labor such an one has done for the Lord has been in vain, for God cannot reward that work and cast the person into the lake of fire. If this possibility exists for any saved person, it surely exists for all and then no one can *know* that his labor is not in vain. But this contradicts Paul's statement, "Ye *know* that your labour is not in vain." Thus to deny the eternal security of the believer makes void God's Word upon which He bases His appeal to steadfastness.

A middle-aged man once admonished a younger man that he should not squander all his money but save some for future days. The young man replied:

"But I might die before I get ready to use it; then it would do me no good." The uncertainty of the future kept that young man from living a steadfast life and in laying up for the future. To the believer, as an incentive to steadfastness and a life abounding in the work of the Lord, God pledges Himself that his work shall not be in vain. The believer's assurance of a life with God throughout all eternity is then the incentive for a steadfast, immovable Christian life on earth which abounds in the work of the Lord. Those who teach Christians that they might be lost are thereby encouraging them to do as the young man did, enjoy the present world for there is no definite assurance that they shall, in the world to come, enjoy the fruits of their labor.

Paul said in this same fifteenth chapter: "If after the manner of men I have fought with beasts at Ephesus, what advantageth it me if the dead rise not? let us eat and drink; for tomorrow we die." And so in measure as Christians, through the denial of eternal security, are being told that they might not be raised to a life of glory with God; are "eating and drinking" in many churches instead of being steadfast, immovable and abounding in the work of the Lord.

Similar appeals to steadfastness are found elsewhere and are based on equally unalterable conditions.

"Therefore, my brethren . . . stand fast in the Lord" (Phil. 4:1). The "therefore" looks back to:

"For our conversation is in heaven; from whence also we look for the Saviour, the Lord Jesus Christ: Who *shall* change our vile body, that it may be fashioned like unto His glorious body, *according to the working whereby He is able even to subdue all things unto Himself*" (Phil. 3:20, 21).

"Therefore, brethren, stand fast, and hold the traditions which ye have been taught, whether by word or our epistle." In this case the "therefore" refers back to "God hath from the beginning chosen you to salvation . . . : whereunto He called you by our gospel to the obtaining of the glory of our Lord Jesus Christ" (2 Thess. 2:15, 13, 14).

The appeal here is based entirely upon God's choosing and calling. There can be no failure in these (see p. 58).

Thus very clearly and definitely God *first gives full assurance to the believer* that he shall be raised from the dead or changed at the last trump; that his vile body shall be fashioned like unto that of the Lord Jesus Christ by the working of the infinite power of God. This is so because God has chosen and He has called by the gospel. It is only after God has made these facts clear that He appeals because of this assurance for steadfast immovable lives abounding in the labor of God.

To deny the eternal security of the believer denies the certainty of that which God makes definite, robs the believer of his assurance thereof and undermines God's appeal.

CONCLUSION

Thus in Chapters XVIII to XXII inclusive, it has been shown that it is that grace of God which brings Salvation that also teaches how to live soberly, righteously and godly in the present world; and it is His eternal love with which He loves, both before the sinner is saved and afterward, that is the dynamic of that life. It is His mercies, as seen in the unalterable standing of the believer in grace, that is the incentive to a full surrender of body and mind to God. It is the believer's high calling in Christ, planned and determined by God before the foundation of the world, and being carried out according to the pleasure of His own will that is the incentive to an earthly life that honors Christ, and is separated from the world. It is the certain knowledge of being transformed into the image of Christ and appearing with Him in glory that is the basis for an appeal to a pure life apart from worldly lusts. The incorruptible, undying nature of the new life of the one who has been born again is given as a reason for desiring to feed upon the Word of God; and finally the assurance of the resurrection of the body, the transformation of the present vile, corruptible body into one fashioned like unto His glorious body is the appeal to be steadfast, immovable, always abounding in the work of the Lord.

Every one of these conditions upon which these various appeals are made demand the eternal security of the ῦeliever. Therefore to teach that it is possible for one who has been saved to be lost is to undermine the very structure of God's argument for a life that is pleasing to Him. Thus the charge that the teaching of eternal security leads to carelessness and a state of low spirituality is not only false; but the teachings against security by those who make this charge are responsible for the conditions for which they blame those who are faithful stewards of the manifold grace of God.

To merely neglect the teaching of these truths is a serious matter.

$$\boxed{23}$$

Can We Know from Experience?

THE ARGUMENTS against eternal security and for the contention that one who has been saved can be lost fall into two broad groups: (1) those based on human observations and reason and (2) those based on Scripture passages interpreted in order to make them so teach. In some arguments both of these errors are intermingled.

Those that are based upon human observations and reasoning shall be considered first. In fact, inasmuch as the subject that is being considered is one that can be known only through divine revelation, all arguments or parts of arguments that are purely on a human level must be ruled out. No evidence can be recognized as such that is not based on God's own revelation. It is well, however, because of the wide acceptance of some of the arguments that are purely human, to show how these arguments deny and contradict God's own Word.

No attempt is made here to deal with all arguments that have been offered against eternal security. Space will not permit nor is it necessary; as

*the case rests not on refutation of human arguments,
but on the positive revelation of God as it is found
in the doctrines of grace.* What follows is offered
to show that the arguments against eternal security
are untenable, and to help some who are bothered
by these arguments.

A very familiar argument of this type is: "We
know from our own experience of persons who have
been saved, but have later been lost." Instances are
also cited of men who have at one time preached the
Gospel, but have later denied God. The human ob-
servation and conclusion drawn therefrom, upon
which this argument is based, may both be incor-
rect, for man is far from infallible. But that is not the
most serious objection to the argument. *Anyone who
definitely makes the statement concerning someone,
that he has been saved and is now lost, is making a
double judgment whereby he intrudes himself into
the position of God.* This is a serious charge, but it
can be sustained by Scripture. Anyone who is saved,
is saved through faith, that is, believing. "He that
heareth My words and believeth Him that sent Me
hath eternal life" (John 5:24 R. V.). Believing is a
heart attitude toward God. "With the heart man believeth unto righteousness" (Rom. 10:10).

What does God say concerning the judgment of
a heart attitude toward Himself? "The Lord seeth
not as man seeth; for man looketh on the outward
appearance, but God looketh on the heart" (1 Sam.
16:7). Thus God specifically says that man cannot
judge as to whether or not a man is at heart right

with Him. Christians ought to recognize others as
Christians, or refuse to recognize them as such in
fellowshipping with them (1 Cor. 5:11 and 2 Thes.
3:6, 14, 15); but this is quite different from making
a positive statement that men are saved or are not
saved. Thus no man can definitely declare of another that he is either saved or lost.

God in His Word has caused to be recorded the
lives of two men, and has also given His own judgment as to whether these men were saved or lost.
In both cases God's judgment is the opposite to
man's, based upon experience.

A favorite sermon subject of a few years ago was,
"Lot Pitched His Tent Toward Sodom." Invariably
it was said that, as a result of this first move toward
Sodom, Lot became a lost man. This surely is the
only conclusion that can be drawn from judging the
experience or the "outward being" of Lot. But those
who so preached entirely overlooked God's testi-
mony concerning Lot which was recorded some two
thousand years after Lot died. It is found in 2 Peter
2:7, 8. "And delivered *just* Lot, vexed with the filthy
conversation of the wicked. (For that *righteous* man
dwelling among them [the people of Sodom], in
seeing and hearing, vexed his *righteous soul* from
day to day with their unlawful deeds)." Man, judging the outward being of Lot, says he was lost. God,
judging his soul, which in Scripture is nearly syn-
onymous with heart, calls him just and righteous.

Who is right, God or man? *No modern case
quoted as proof against eternal security has looked*

more hopeless than Lot. Yet men who are teachers
of God's Word say, "We know from our own experience that persons who have been saved can be lost."

Let no one condemn this reference to the life of
Lot nor say that it should not be mentioned, as it
encourages sinful living. The fact that God has had
it recorded in His Word is authority for its use.
When properly understood, the life of Lot becomes
a tremendous warning, in the most concrete terms
possible, of what it means to be saved so as by fire.
This warning is entirely lost when it is used to warn
saved people of the supposed possibility of their
being lost. Lot's life is placed in contrast to that of
Abraham. To both, righteousness was imputed
apart from works. Surely no Christian would choose
the life of Lot with its barrenness and ultimate loss
of everything except life itself, when it is possible
to have a life like that of Abraham to whom God revealed His purposes and who was called the friend
of God.

The other person in God's record is one whom
man's judgment calls saved, but God said that he
was lost. It is Judas Iscariot. Judas is the ever present proof to many for the possibility of being saved
and later lost. Read his life. He was numbered as
one of the twelve earthly disciples of Jesus. He was
so trusted by the others that he was made their
treasurer. He was with the twelve when they were
sent out to preach the gospel of the Kingdom. There
is not the slightest record of any of the other eleven
mistrusting him. He was included in the "we" when

Peter said, "We believe and are sure that Thou art the Christ, the Son of the living God" (John 6:69). Surely from experience, Peter and the other disciples thought they knew that Judas was saved.

But when Peter made that great confession of faith in Christ, which in itself is the very basis for being saved (John 3:36), and included in it Judas, Jesus *immediately* challenged it by saying, "One of you is a devil." What made this difference in judgment? Peter knew only the outward being of Judas —Jesus Christ knew his heart.

Again, after Jesus had washed the disciples' feet, He was very careful when He said, "Ye are clean" to add, "but not all. For He knew who should betray Him; therefore said He, Ye are not all clean" (John 13:11). Jesus had washed the feet of Judas as well as the others. Therefore, the difference between Judas and the others was that he had not been bathed (v. 10 R. V.); hence he was not clean. This is the washing (the same root word as is used for bathed in John 13:10) of regeneration (Tit. 3:5) by which Judas had *not* been cleansed. As this bath is a "once for all" cleansing (Heb. 10:1-12), Judas had never been saved, according to the record of the Scripture.

In the days of the early Church, there were those among the true believers who went out from among them. Of them it is written: "They went out from us, but they were not of us; for if they had been of us, they would have continued with us, but they went out that they might be made manifest that they all are not of us (1 John 2:19 R. V.). As the very purpose of their going out was to manifest (make known) that they were not of the saved, it is clear that they had been fully recognized as saved.

Finally then, the one who says, "We know from our own experience that there are those who have been saved but are lost," places his own observations and judgment above God's statements to the contrary. But that is not all, he allows his own limited human observations and judgments to deny what God teaches in all the doctrines of the grace of God, which, it has been shown, demand the eternal security of the believer for their full understanding and acceptance. *It is placing fallible and finite judgments and reasoning of man above God's infinite and infallible Word.*

24

Is Man a Free Moral Agent?

THOSE WHO reject the doctrine of the eternal security of the believer rest heavily on the argument that man is a free moral agent, and, as such can, after he has been saved, will to go away from God and become lost just as he had previously willed to come to God and be saved. This is one of their strongest arguments.

Space does not permit an exhaustive discussion of the free moral agency of man, nor is it necessary. All that is needed is to show the error of the argument as presented.

There are at least four separate and distinct fallacies in this one argument: (1) Man can reverse his freedom of action and its effects at pleasure; (2) Being a free moral agent, man is a free agent in other matters; (3) That man is a free moral agent in respect to salvation; (4) That the sovereign grace of God is limited by the free moral agency of man.

1. IS MAN FREE TO REVERSE HIS ACTIONS AND THEIR EFFECTS AT PLEASURE?

It is argued that because man can come to God and be saved, he can therefore will to go away from God and be lost. In other words, he can reverse his action and thereby reverse the effects thereof. If it can be shown that there are conditions under which the effects of voluntary acts of man cannot be reversed by the free will of man, then the argument falls for no other proof is ever offered to support the statement that man can go away from God and be lost. There surely is no revelation from God in this matter and nothing less than that has any weight.

To Adam was given freedom to eat or not to eat of the tree of knowledge of good and evil. He was therefore in the true sense, a free moral agent. He ate of the fruit in disobedience to God's command and as a result, became a sinner and his nature became sinful. Because of this sinful nature, he, as well as the whole human race, lost that state of being a free moral agent with ability either to obey or disobey God's commandment. No one of Adam's seed has ever been able to fully obey God's law. Not one has by a voluntary deed been able to reverse the effects of Adam's act committed by him as a free moral agent.

Again, a woman may be a free agent in the matter of entering into marriage relations with a man. But thereafter, the Bible clearly states, she is bound by the law of the husband as long as he lives (Rom. 7:2).

These two citations prove conclusively that freedom to act along a given line does not imply freedom to reverse that action and the effects thereof. It surely does not then follow, that because one has willed to come to God and be saved, he can will to go away and be lost.

2. A FREE MORAL AGENT IS NOT A FREE AGENT.

A free moral agent is a "being capable of those actions . . . which can properly be denominated good or evil in a moral sense." There are matters outside of the moral realm in which a free moral agent is not a free agent. The contention that one who has been saved can go away from God and be lost because such a one is a free moral agent, ascribes a power to will and act far greater than can possibly be included under the free moral agency of man. In fact, it really makes man, who is only a creature, an entirely free agent independent of his Creator and Saviour.

No man ever willed to be born into the human race, and equally impotent is he to will to separate himself from the human race and become something else or even nothing at all. He may, by suicide, shorten his earthly existence, but he is still in the human race and shall be called as a man out of his grave. In this, he is clearly not a free agent. Yet it is argued that a saved man can will to separate himself from God. His entry into the kingdom of God was by birth. He was "born of God" into that state. It was not of his own will, for one who is "born of God" is born *"not of the will of man"* (John 1:13). It is true that the unsaved man wills to come to God, but it is not the *willing to come* to God that places him in the kingdom of God. That is by an act of God. Man has as little to do with that as he had to do with his physical birth. As it is impossible for man, by free action, to separate himself from the human race, so it is equally impossible for him, by a free act, to separate himself from God's kingdom. To whatever degree man may be a free moral agent, that freedom is exercised entirely within the limits of his humanity. There is no such thing as free moral agency of man within the kingdom of God, for those who are born of God *cannot* sin (1 John 3:9). They have a divine nature which is in harmony with God. (See also p. 50.)

Clearly, then, the contention that man is a free moral agent does not include the freedom to will to go away from Christ and God. Truly, once a son of mankind, always a son of mankind, and equally true, once a child of God, always a child of God. There is no possibility for a man, by his own will or action, to change either of these two conditions. As man cannot change this condition and God will not, for Jesus said: "Him that cometh to Me, I will in no wise cast out" (John 6:37); all who are saved are secure for all eternity.

3. IS MAN A FREE MORAL AGENT WITH REFERENCE TO SALVATION?

To say that man is a free moral agent and, as such, can come to God and be saved; and can, therefore, go away and thereby be lost, implies that man is saved or lost, due to his own actions as a free moral agent. The argument, as it is stated, does not leave room for any other cause of salvation than the free agency of man. No other power greater than that of man as a free moral agent could possibly contribute to salvation, if the power of man as a free agent can set it aside.

As a free moral agent is a being capable of good and evil actions, necessarily to be saved, such a being must always do that which is good.

Adam was created "good" and was made a free moral agent. He and Eve before the fall, were the only members of the human race that could truly be called free moral agents. But Adam (and this includes Eve) exercised his free moral agency by disobeying God's commandment, and thereby was placed under the condemnation of that commandment. This condemnation is death and everyone descended from Adam is in the same position, for death passed upon all men. The unsaved are described as dead in trespasses and sins; and are energized by Satan as children of disobedience (Eph. 2:1, 2). They are blinded by the god of this world (2 Cor. 3:14). Not until God has shined in their hearts by the convicting ministry of the Holy Spirit (John 16:7-11) can they intelligently exercise saving faith. *No man can come to* Jesus Christ *except* the *Father draws* him (John 6:44). This is God's picture of man. Is that the picture of a free moral agent *who can will* to come to God and be saved? Scarcely!

Notice that the free moral agency of Adam was in the matter of obeying or disobeying God's law. Through Adam's disobedience, his nature became sinful and that sinful nature, by the law of birth, was passed on to all men. This sinful nature makes man incapable of those actions that are good in a degree demanded by God's law, and therefore though he is still a moral agent, he is not a *free* moral agent. Paul, speaking of his old nature which came from Adam, said: "I am carnal, sold under sin." He also said: "The good that I would, I do not; but the evil which I would not, that I do." He saw himself brought into captivity to a law of sin which was in his members (Rom. 7:14, 19, 20, 23). This is the true picture of the Adamic nature of every man—every so-called free moral agent. Because of this, it could be said: "All have sinned and come short of the glory of God" (Rom. 3:23). Only One has been able to "refuse the evil and choose the good" (Isa. 7:15). He was the Seed of the woman and not of the sinful seed of Adam.

Thus it is impossible for man by any free action on his part so to live that he is good in the sight of God's holy law. In other words, man cannot be justified by the works of the law. He is not saved by any good action that he may take as a free moral agent.

If a man is not saved through his acts as a free moral agent, then the conclusion that he can go away from God and be lost, certainly does not follow. Thus for the third time the argument has been shown to be fallacious.

4. IS THE SOVEREIGN GRACE OF GOD
LIMITED BY MAN'S WILL?

To say that man can will to go away from God

and be lost is to make the sovereign grace of God subject to the will of man. This must be so because it is clearly revealed that grace reigns unto eternal life (Rom. 5:21). If man can will to go away from God and be lost, then grace does not reign unto life —grace is not sovereign. To many there seems to be a clash between the so-called free moral agency of man and the sovereign grace of God. This is not true.

As has been shown, after Adam had sinned, man was no longer a free moral agent in the sense that he was able to do good and thereby fulfill the demands of God's holy law. Therefore, because of the demands of God's righteousness, man is lost. But God made a special provision whereby man can satisfy the demands of God's righteousness as expressed in His holy law.

This provision is in the person of His Own Son Who paid the death penalty of the broken law. This being done, God again gave man freedom to will. This second freedom to will is with respect to His Son. Man can either reject or accept Him. Those who reject Him remain in the position of being guilty and under the condemnation of the law. The one who accepts Him as the One Who paid the penalty of the law for him, through faith, establishes God's law. The law is thus held inviolate and God's righteousness is vindicated. Each and everyone who so accepts Christ acts as a free agent under God's commandment.

It has already been pointed out that when Adam exercised his freedom and broke God's commandment, he thereby became possessor of a sinful nature which made it impossible for him to act freely and be restored to his former state. So also by contrast, when one has of his own free will accepted Christ as the propitiation which satisfies the demands of God's holy law, he is given a *new divine nature* which makes it impossible for him to will to return to his former state.

It is at this point that man's free agency in the matter of fulfilling God's law comes to an end. In fact, by so acting as a free agent, man confesses that he is not a *free moral* agent. By accepting Christ as the propitiation for his sins, a man admits that he is not free to do good himself and thus satisfy God's law.

It is also at this very point, when man exercises saving faith, that the sovereignty of grace begins to operate. Until a man has accepted Christ and thereby established God's law, he is under the demands of God's righteousness. When these demands are satisfied, the floodgates of grace are opened and grace becomes sovereign and reigns unto eternal life (Rom. 5:21). It is, therefore, the righteousness of God that limits the sovereignty of His grace. Man, by accepting God's provision for satisfaction of His own righteousness, places himself at the mercy seat where nothing but the grace of God can touch him. Thus, man's freedom of will is related to God's holy law and ceases to exist in the matter of life or death (saved or lost) when the sovereignty of grace begins.

Surely nothing can be ascribed to the free moral agency of man that can in the slightest interfere with the operation of the sovereign grace of God which guarantees the eternal life of every one who has been saved.

Is any further proof needed to show the unbiblical position of the argument based on the free moral agency of man?

25

Some Arguments Answered

Answers to many of the arguments against eternal security have been given throughout the preceding pages. These answers need not be repeated here, but it might be helpful to some to have the arguments mentioned and references made to the pages where answers to them can be found.

One of the most familiar arguments against eternal security and one that meets with much sympathetic reception is the statement: "To teach that a saved person is eternally secure and cannot be lost causes worldliness in the church and loss of spiritual power." This argument is not only answered in Chapters XVIII-XXII; but it has been shown that denial of the security of the saved one robs God's appeals for a holy and godly life of their force, and thus it is in fact those who oppose the doctrine of eternal security who are responsible for that condition.

Another criticism is that young people, who go away from home and are taught eternal security at a Bible institute or conference, come back and enthusiastically, but unwisely, spread the doctrine in their home church. On pages 10 and 11, it is pointed out that the responsibility for this condition rests upon those who have been responsible for the Bible training in that church, because they have failed to teach properly the doctrines of the grace of God.

The statement that, while Christ will not cast out one that comes to Him, it is possible for a saved person voluntarily to go away from God, has no basis whatever in Scripture. It is purely human imagination and cannot be accepted as an argument to decide a question, the only known facts of which are to be found in God's own revelation. That it is impossible for a saved person to go away from God is shown on pages 119 and 120.

The argument that a sheep can jump out of God's hand and be lost is also of this same class. No direct statement from the Bible has ever been offered to sustain it. The only authority back of it is the reasoning of the fallible human being that makes it. The impossibility of such action is shown on pages 3 and 4. As the freedom of man's will is here involved, the answer to the last preceding argument applies here also.

It is argued that while eternal life is eternal, it is possible for a saved person to lose that eternal life, and that under certain conditions (which are never clearly defined), God will take back the eternal life unto Himself. This argument entirely ignores God's revelation concerning the new birth. (See Chapter XXIX.) It would be just as reasonable to say that a mother can take back unto herself the life that she has given to her child. Furthermore, it has been shown (p. 30) that eternal life is a gift from God and that He never repents having given it.

It is often said that a saved person can lose the Holy Spirit. This is a direct denial of John 14:16, which clearly states that He abides forever.

It has been argued that as the physical life can be starved until it dies so also the spiritual, if it is not fed, will starve to death. This is offered as proof that a saved person can be lost. The fallacy in this argument is that comparison is made between two absolutely dissimilar things: physical life and the life that comes through the new birth. That physical life is universally mortal (subject to death) is clearly taught in the Bible. Death has passed upon all men (Rom. 5:12). But that spiritual life, which is given to one who is born again, is of God said to be eternal. This it must be, for it is of incorruptible seed "which liveth and abideth forever" (1 Pet. 1:23). To compare these two kinds of life and say that they are similar in this essential respect is to contradict God's declaration that they are diametrically different.

It is contended that of the two views, it is more reasonable to hold that one who has been saved can be lost. That statement can be freely granted, but it must be remembered that that which springs from a loving heart is not the result of reason, even when on a human plane. Salvation is altogether unreasonable. Why should God give His only begotten Son, and why should that Son voluntarily give His life that man, who had rebelled against Him and was worthy of nothing else than everlasting separation from Him might throughout all eternity live—not as restored to the originally perfect state in which he was created—but as a being like the Son Himself, higher than all others of God's created beings? Salvation is all of love and mercy. Where then is there any room to argue the reasonableness of any part of

God's plan of salvation? In the light of God's own revelation of His infinite love, the argument from human reason instantly fades into nothingness. It is, however, most unreasonable to accept God's revelation concerning His love and sacrifice in saving a person, and then deny that He "Who worketh all things after the counsel of His own will" (Eph. 1:11), has not provided for the keeping of that for which He has sacrificed so much.

But why weary the reader by multiplying refutations of these purely human arguments? Enough has been given to demonstrate that these arguments are without support in God's Word. In fact, are contrary to it. Nor, as has already been said, does the proof of the controversy lie in answering all such arguments that the human mind might conceive. The real proof is in God's own revelation which has been presented at considerable length. It is, as someone has said: "We are not governed by reason but by revelation."

As a help to those who have been confused by what has been offered as biblical proof against eternal security, a few more arguments will be answered. Certain "musts" are imposed upon those who are saved in order to remain saved. Two will be mentioned. It is said that a believer is secure as long as he remains in Christ, but he must remain in Christ or he shall be lost. For a consideration of this "must," the writer is referred to pp. 161 and 162.

Another is, "the saved person must continue to believe." If he ceases to believe he is lost. Few who make this statement realize that if this is true, then a

saved person is lost the instant he harbors a doubt.
One argument which is hardly worthy of recogni-
tion, except for the fact that it has been quite freely
used in certain quarters, is that the ending -*eth* of
believeth makes the word mean continuous believing. If this be true, then all verbs ending in -*eth* also
signify continuous and incompleted action. It is suggested that the reader try this out by reading John
4:5, 7 and 13 and 11:28, 38. But there are some who
are truly concerned about this point. For those, assurance will be found in John 5:24 R. V. "Verily,
verily, I say unto you, He that heareth My Word,
and believeth Him that sent Me, hath eternal life,
and cometh not into judgment, but hath passed out
of death into life." This verse makes it clear that saving faith is not a process, but an act. *Anything that is
brought to pass by a process cannot be spoken of as
accomplished as long as the need for the process
continues. When a thing has been accomplished,
then that through which it was brought to pass is no
further needed.* In this verse eternal life (which cannot end) is said to have been given. It is not being
given. It is also stated that "he that believeth *has*
(already) passed (past tense) from death unto life."
Salvation from the penalty of sin, that is from the
condemnation of the law, is by no means a process;
it is an instantaneous act of God in response to a
single act of faith on the part of the sinner.

It is taught in Ephesians 1:13, 14, that after a person has believed (a finished act) he is sealed with
the Holy Spirit until the redemption of the purchased possession. This passage once and for all

rules out the argument that one must continue to believe.

There is a need for continuous faith on the part of the saved person; but that is not in relation to the question of eternal life (being saved) or everlasting condemnation (being lost), and therefore is not a part of this discussion.

It is said that sin in the life of a saved person will result in that one's being lost. There are not many who are willing to go so far as to say that any sin whatsoever will cause a saved person to be lost, especially if they are reminded that, "whatsoever is not of faith is sin," and "to him that knoweth to do good, and doeth it not, to him it is sin" (Rom. 14:23 and Jas. 4:17). In fact anything that comes short of the glory of God is sin (Rom. 3:23). Yet it is maintained that there are certain kinds of sins: unconfessed sins, willful sins, or continued sinning that will result in the one who commits them being lost. *To accept this condition is to acknowledge that there are degrees of sin. It is to say that there are sins which a saved person can commit and still remain saved, but there are others which must be avoided or one shall be lost.* To make this concrete, the following list of sins is given: an unkind thought, a slight snub of a fellow Christian, a bit of envy because someone else has been more highly honored, a hasty unkind word, a misrepresentation of someone else, a white lie, pride, envy, jealousy, resentment to another, a root of bitterness, greed, hatred, wrath, strife, theft, falsification, idolatry, drunkenness, revellings, fornication, adultery, murder. From

the above list, which sins can be safely committed
and which not? Where is the line to be drawn and
by whom? And where is the Bible authority for the
classification when it is finished? Those who contend against eternal security are unwilling to state
clearly their position in this matter. They are not as
frank as is the Roman Church which classifies sins
as venial and mortal.

But one need not be bewildered by this indefinite
presentation of the sin question. God in the death of
Christ made an absolute and full provision for sin
and satisfied all the demands of His law. This has
already been explained in Chapters VIII and IX,
and need not be repeated here.

And this leads on to the next argument: "If a
saved person cannot be lost, what of backsliders?"
This word is greatly misunderstood. In the first
place, the word never occurs in relation to the saved
of the Church age. It is exclusively an Old Testament word and, with one exception (Prov. 14:14
which is a different word in the original), is applied
nationally to Israel and Judah. As the things that are
recorded concerning God's chosen people Israel, are
examples to believers of this age (1 Cor. 10:6), it
seems entirely proper to speak of a saved person
who has departed from a life of obedience to God as
a backslider. *But when this is done, to be consistent,
such persons must necessarily be considered in the
same light as God considered His Old Testament
backsliding people.*

In connection with the first mention of backsliding, it is written: "Thine own wickedness shall cor-

rect thee, and thy *backslidings shall reprove* thee" (Jer. 2:19). Reproof then is connected with back-slidings. This at once suggests chastening through which God corrects those saved persons who do not judge themselves (see p. 62).

In the next chapter are found these words, "Turn, O backsliding children, saith the Lord; for I am married unto you" (Jer. 3:14). Here the Lord speaks of that which He regards as an unbreakable tie. Then follows a prophecy of that restoration of Judah and Israel to their own land which has not yet been fulfilled. Then in verse 22 is a loving entreaty: "Return, ye backsliding children, I will heal your backslidings," and they answer: "Behold, we are come unto Thee; for Thou art Jehovah [the redemptive Name for God] our God."

In this passage surely there can be found nothing on which to base the statement that a backslider is lost. On the contrary, it teaches that a backslider is in an inseparable relation to God and shall be restored.

In a second message God says (Jer. 5:6) of Judah, "Their backslidings are increased"; and then tells of what another writer calls chastenings, "with the rod of men, and with the stripes of the children of men" (2 Sam. 7:14) that are to come over them; but also adds: "Nevertheless . . . I will not make a full end with you" (v. 18). Yet again God pleads: "Why then is this people of Jerusalem slidden back by a perpetual backsliding?" and again more chastenings are predicted. They shall be melted and tried (Jer. 9:7); they shall be fed with wormwood, and given gall to drink (v. 15). The student of history well knows how hard the rod has been and how severe the stripes; how they have been melted by the fires of persecution and how bitter the wormwood and gall. It has all been chastening, but not everlasting separation.

More than six hundred years later, it was written: "Hath God cast away His people? God forbid . . . God hath not cast away His people which He foreknew" (Rom. 11:1, 2). "And so all Israel shall be saved" (v. 26) because "as touching the election they are beloved for the fathers' sakes" (v. 28).

And so also the backslider, while chastened by the Lord, is in no wise cast out (John 6:37), because he also is "elect according to the foreknowledge of God" (1 Pet. 1:2). "For the gifts and calling of God are without repentance" (Rom. 11:29).

While here is comfort, there is also a warning of the most solemn kind. God's mercies can not be trifled with. One who trifles with the grace of God, though not lost, because salvation is of grace, shall suffer the just consequences of his sins.

Thus the case of the backslider, when considered in the bright light of God's own revelation instead of in the dim light of human reason, becomes a strong and intensely specific argument for eternal security. Nor is that all, it contradicts the charge that those who accept eternal security teach that it makes no difference how a saved one lives.

26

Why the Warnings?

IT IS argued: if a saved person cannot be lost, why then all the warnings in the Bible? So to question is to imply that all warnings are addressed to saved persons and the only thing about which God needs to warn those who are saved is that they do not do something to cause Him to condemn them to everlasting death. Is there then nothing else for an individual about which God is concerned than the matter of eternal life or everlasting condemnation?

There are many warnings addressed to believers but, before considering some of them, it might be well to discuss briefly some warnings which are often taken to apply to Christians but really do not directly apply to them.

Some of these passages in which certain individuals are warned are addressed to others than the saved of this age. In Matthew 24:42 and Mark 13:14, are warnings to servants to watch. In both, it is clearly said that this watchfulness is in the expectation of the coming of the "Son of Man" (Matt. 24:37 and Mark 13:34). Speaking of this coming, Matthew 24:30 says: "Then shall all the tribes of the earth mourn, and they shall see the Son of Man coming in the clouds of heaven with power and great glory," and according to verse 29, this shall take place immediately after the great tribulation. As the Church is taken up before the tribulation, these passages cannot, in their primary sense, be applied to present-day believers.

It is to be noted also that these warnings are to "servants." Jesus in speaking to His disciples said, "Henceforth I call you not servants . . . but I have called you friends" (John 15:15). Under the law, God's people in their activity for Him are servants, but under grace they are "friends." Thus it is doing violence to the new relationship to say that these passages apply to Christians.

Another passage in which there is a warning that is made to apply to saved persons is Hebrews 6:1-9. This is discussed elsewhere at considerable length (see p. 147). This warning is directed against the possibility of Jews in the early groups of Jewish Christians trusting in the sufficiency of a ceremonial worship and the kingdom teachings, but without a personal faith in the Saviour indispensable to salvation. There are large numbers in the churches today who have the form of godliness, but do not know the power thereof. These, who are mere professors but not true believers, are warned by passages such as this one. There is a special need today to warn the unsaved within the churches. By applying to Christians warnings as this one, is to rob that class of persons who need so sadly the warning of God's Word to them.

Throughout the pages of the Bible are found records of the mixture of tares with the wheat. From the days of the mixed multitude that went with Israel out of Egypt to the false teachers of the Church age who transform themselves into apostles of Christ (2 Cor. 11:13; 2 Pet. 2:1 and 1 John 4:1), there has been need of warnings to God's people to distinguish between those who are truly His own and those who are not. Here then is one great reason for the warnings in the Bible.

As great as is the matter of eternal life, God most certainly has much more than this for the one that He has saved from the penalty of sin and, through the new birth, has placed in His own Kingdom. If that were all, why does He not take those who are saved unto Himself immediately after they are saved? Certainly one who has been purchased at so great a price as the blood of His own Son would not be left on earth at the risk of being lost if he could be lost, and also without any purpose for that earthly life!

But God has a purpose for the earthly life of those that are blood bought, and it is in relation to this purpose that the warnings are addressed to believers.

THE FRUITS OF THE EARTHLY LIFE MIGHT BE LOST

It is terribly possible for one who has received eternal life, whose spirit has been saved, to suffer loss of all that might have been accomplished by his earthly life. Every man's work (the sum total of his earthly life) shall be tested by fire. "If any man's work shall be burned, he shall suffer loss; but he himself shall be saved; yet so as by fire" (1 Cor. 3:12-15).

In line with this, the writer of Hebrews says: "Wherefore we receiving a kingdom which cannot be moved, let us have grace whereby we may serve God acceptably with reverence and godly fear: for our God is a consuming fire" (Heb. 12:28, 29). A similar warning is found in 2 Corinthians 5:10-11. Lot is the outstanding example of such a person. All the works of his life were lost in Sodom. Even upon those of the city who were nearest to him was his influence lost. Certainly no Christian wants to be saved as was Lot when he might be like Abraham. A first need for the warnings to saved persons then is the possibility of the loss of the fruits of the earthly life.

WARNINGS AGAINST LOSS OF INFLUENCE

A second need for warnings to saved persons, which is really a part of the one just mentioned, but important enough to justify special mention, is the ever present possibility of a Christian losing his influence in the world for God.

The possibility of salt losing its savour and being cast out and trodden under foot of *man* (Matt. 5:13) is used as a warning of this type. So also is the possibility of a man withering as a branch and being cast by *men* into the fire (John 15:6).

One of the most searching warnings of this kind is found in Revelation 2:5: "Remember therefore from whence thou art fallen, and repent, and do the first works; or else I will come unto thee quickly, and will remove thy candlestick out of his place, except thou repent." This warning is addressed to the angel of the church at Ephesus. This church had stood as a great light bearer surrounded by dark heathenism and even at the time the warning was spoken, much good was said about this church; but it had left its "first love" and therefore the warning. How sensitive God is in the matter of letting His light shine out through those who are His own! All through the centuries of the Church age, the pages of history are filled with records of churches and individual men that have been discarded by God as light bearers in this world of darkness. To interpret this warning as a possibility of being lost is to rob that church (or individual) which is very actively engaged in God's work and zealous for the faith once delivered unto the saints, of the much needed warning that an essential to being a light bearer is a personal love for the Lord.

REWARDS MIGHT BE LOST

God will reward in eternity those who have been saved and who serve Him faithfully during their earthly life. "If any man's work abide . . . he shall receive a reward" (1 Cor. 3:14). But it is also possible for a man to lose that reward which God had made possible for him to gain and He solemnly warns of this: "Hold fast that which thou hast, that no man take thy crown" (Rev. 3:11). Crowns are rewards for faithfulness to God. They do not represent eternal life. This is perfectly clear from Revelation 4:4 to 11, which depicts the scene wherein the twenty-four elders cast their crowns before the throne saying, "Thou art worthy, O Lord, to receive glory and honour and power." There is a glory and honor for eternity that can be lost and God warns His children as to the possibility of losing it.

WARNINGS TO AVOID CHASTENING

Thus far only warnings as to loss or gain for eternity have been considered. There are also warnings that consider the present life of the believer. While it is true that every child of God is subject to chastening, it is also true that the amount of chastening may be more or less, depending upon the believer's judgment of himself for allowing sin in his life. Those who do not judge themselves are warned that God will judge and chasten them. (1 Cor. 11:27-32).

IT IS POSSIBLE NOT TO ENTER INTO REST

The Lord Jesus Christ said: "Come unto Me, all ye that labour and are heavy laden, and I will give you rest" (Matt. 11:28). What can be meant by this rest? It is the rest that He gives to all who have labored with the heavy burden of sin, which He through His death takes away from all who have come to Him, confessing themselves as sinners. It is a rest in His finished work of salvation.

That this is a rest to be enjoyed during this earthly life is clear from the words that follow: "Take My yoke upon you, and learn of Me."

There are many Christians who do not have this rest because they do not understand that when Jesus Christ died on the cross, God performed through Him a finished work of salvation which is theirs through simply coming to Him in faith. Instead of resting in the finished work of Christ, they are constantly laboring in order to be accepted of God. They are trying to be justified by their own efforts. They are always struggling to "hold out" but have no rest—no assurance—that they shall see Christ in glory.

God has given a solemn warning against just this condition, but the warning has to a large extent been lost because the passage has been made to mean the possible loss of eternal life.

This warning is found in Hebrews 4:1-3: "Let us fear, therefore, lest haply, a promise being left of entering into His rest, any one of you should seem to have come short of it. For indeed we have had good tidings preached unto us, even as also they: but the word of hearing did not profit them, because it was not united by faith with them that heard. For we who have believed do enter into that rest" (R. V.). The interpretation which makes this passage teach that a saved person can be lost and thus fail to enter into rest in heaven overlooks the present tense of the words: "For we who have believed do [not shall] enter into that rest." The tenth verse makes this even more definite for there the entering into rest is already an accomplished fact. "For he that is entered into His rest hath himself also rested from his works, as God did from His." And here it is clearly said that the rest is from one's own works.

Those who use this passage to deny the eternal security of the believer and add works as a condition for salvation are responsible for the failure of many Christians to cease from their own works and to enter into that rest which comes from faith in the finished work of Christ.

While there are many other warnings in the Bible, enough have been considered to show the emptiness of the argument, "Why then the warnings, if a saved person cannot be lost?", and also the shallowness of the interpretation of the Bible which denies eternal security.

27

Misinterpreted Bible Passages

A CONSIDERABLE NUMBER of Scripture passages are offered as arguments against eternal security. These are selected from various parts of the Bible and are given interpretations which show that one who has been saved can be lost.

The basic principle of Bible study and interpretation is that *the Bible is one great, harmonious presentation of truth and that each part must harmonize with every other part and with the whole. The great truths concerning sin and condemnation, and grace and eternal life, are outlines to which all else must conform. Therefore the doctrines of sin and of the grace of God are the background against which individual verses must be examined. If there is an apparent meaning that contradicts these great doctrines, then it is necessary to seek some other meaning. Even if no other meaning seems possible, such a verse or even several such cannot be made to annul all that is taught by the whole body of harmonious truth which outweighs such individual verses a thousand fold.*

The only God-honoring practice is to accept the divine revelation of the large body of truth and humbly seek a meaning that is in harmony therewith for the few individual, difficult verses. To do otherwise is to rob God's Word of its power to give comfort, joy and assurance.

Interpretations given to passages to make them contradict the eternal security of the believer are subject to various errors that might well be considered under four different groups:

1. Applying to the saved, passages addressed to others.

2. Interpreting passages apart from their context.

3. Difficult, or obscure, passages wrongly interpreted.

4. Using passages in figurative language to formulate a doctrine.

Only a part of the passages that are offered to prove that a saved person can be lost can be considered here. Those considered will, however, be sufficient in number to illustrate clearly the various errors of interpretation. Nor is it necessary in all cases to give a full and correct interpretation of each passage quoted. For the purpose of this discussion, all that is needed is to show a good reason why any given passage cannot mean that one who has been saved can be lost.

1. APPLYING TO THE SAVED PASSAGES ADDRESSED TO OTHERS

"When a righteous man doth turn from his righteousness, and commit iniquity, and I lay a stumblingblock before him, he shall die" (Ezk. 3:20). This was true under the law, but the saved one is "not under the law, but under grace" (Rom.

6:14), and therefore it cannot apply to him. Every saved person has been justified (reckoned righteous) through the redemption that is in Christ Jesus (Rom. 3:24) and does not stand before God in his own righteousness.

"The soul that sinneth, it shall die" (Ezk. 18:4, 20). This also is under the law. Under grace, the saved one is already dead in the person of his Substitute, Jesus Christ (2 Cor. 5:14), and is free from the condemnation (death penalty) of the law.

Matthew 18:23-35. This passage is under law. The principle for forgiveness which applies to the Christian is found in Ephesians 4:32: ". . . forgiving one another, even as God for Christ's sake has forgiven you."

"But he that shall endure unto the end shall be saved" (Matt. 24:13). This is said of Israel passing through the great tribulation and cannot be applied to Christians. The same is true of Mark 13:13. The context in each case shows this clearly.

The person referred to in Luke 11:24-26, into whom the evil spirit reenters, cannot be one who has been born again, for every such person is indwelt by the Holy Spirit, Who abides forever (John 14:16, 17). He cannot, therefore, be said to be an empty house. That individual was merely reformed —not regenerated.

"Now the Spirit speaketh expressly, that in the latter times some shall depart from the faith, giving heed to seducing spirits, and doctrines of devils" (1 Tim. 4:1). This passage does not speak of the individual's faith in the Saviour for salvation. Those spoken of here teach doctrines of devils instead of doctrines of faith which the Church has taught. In 1 John 2:18, 19, these same persons are mentioned, and there it is clearly stated that "they went out, that it might be made manifest that they *were not of us*." Hence, they have never been saved, even though they have passed as believers and represented themselves as such. There are several passages that speak of false teachers who are a part of the apostasy of these last days. They have departed from the faith held by their fathers in the Church. Thus to depart from the faith does not require a previous, personal faith in Christ as is necessary to be saved.

2. PASSAGES INTERPRETED APART FROM THE CONTEXT

Some very serious errors are made by using certain passages entirely apart from their context to show that one who has been saved can be lost. "Ye are fallen from grace" (Gal. 5:4) is quoted as a sure proof that a saved person can be lost. This statement is made to describe a Christian who has fallen into sin. If those who so use this statement will take time to read the entire verse, they will see how far they miss the true meaning. It is not those who fall into sin, but those who are particularly concerned with doing everything that the *law* requires in order to be righteous in God's sight, so as to remain saved that are fallen from grace. *Thus it is they themselves who insist upon works to remain*

saved who have fallen from grace. To apply the
by-works principle to the unsaved is to be guilty of
preaching another gospel (Gal. 1:8-9). To apply
it to believers is to encourage them to fall from
grace.

The theme of Galatians is "Having begun in the
Spirit, are ye made perfect by the flesh?" It is not a
treatise on the new birth as John 3:1-21, nor on
salvation from the penalty of sin as Ephesians
2:1-10. It is an appeal to a life in the liberty of grace
instead of in the bondage of the law.

Another favorite statement used entirely apart
from its context to prove that a saved person can
be lost is found in Hebrews 6:6. It consists of these
five words: "If they shall fall away." It is said that
this shows clearly the possibility of a Christian being
lost. What is the context? Verses 4-6 are all one
sentence that speaks of persons who have had certain experiences which are mentioned. It is true that
in the words, "if they shall fall away," it is implied
that it is possible to fall away from that which had
been experienced, but *the essential statement concerning these persons,* whoever they may be, *is:*
"For it is impossible . . . if they fall away, *to renew
them again unto repentance."* If the words, "if they
shall fall away," refer to persons that have been
saved, so must also the words, "It is impossible . . .
to renew them again unto repentance." Do those
who make the implied meaning prove that a saved
person can be lost also accept and teach that one
who has thus become lost, cannot be renewed unto
repentance? *They do not.* They are always urging

backsliders to come and be saved again. This is an excellent illustration of the shallowness of much of the teaching against eternal security.

That this statement is not made concerning believers is made clear by verse 9. "But we are persuaded *better* things [than those mentioned] of you, *and things that accompany salvation.*" Thus these persons cannot be said to have been saved. Who then were they? This explanation is suggested. The letter is written to the Hebrews. Read the first three verses of the chapter and notice how perfectly they describe Nicodemus who came to Jesus by night. Yet Jesus refused to be addressed by him as a "Teacher come from God," but told him that *he needed to be born again.* While with Jesus, Nicodemus entered into those things which are mentioned in verses 4 and 5. Had Nicodemus gone away from Jesus and "fallen away" from all that he received there, then he could not have been renewed unto repentance, for he would have gone back and continued to try to establish his own righteousness, as did the other Jews of whom Paul writes in Romans 10:1-3. Thus this passage refers to Jews passing from under the covenant of the law into salvation and cannot be said to be concerning saved persons.

Hebrews 10:26-29, 39 is a similar passage.

3. OBSCURE PASSAGES WRONGLY INTERPRETED

A third error in the use of Scripture passages to deny the eternal security of the believer is to interpret wrongly passages, the meaning of which depends upon the meaning of some word or phrase in the passage. A favorite passage of this class is 1 Corinthians 9:27. In *Voices from the Silent Centuries,* Dr. Harry Rimmer has the following to say concerning this passage. It is here quoted with his consent:

"Strange as it may seem, however, there are some who do not care to rest in the security of the finished work of Christ, and these reject the provisions of the doctrine of Grace; contending that we are safe only as long as we are able to keep ourselves. This school of thought would have us saved one day and lost the next, losing sight of the gracious promise of Jesus, 'I GIVE unto them eternal life, and they SHALL NEVER PERISH.' Pressed for some verse of Scripture on which to base their unhappy doctrine, they generally refer to 1 Corinthians 9:27. Here Paul writes, 'But I keep my body under, and bring it into subjection: lest by any means, when I have preached to others I myself should be a castaway.' This implies, according to these mistaken friends, that Paul was afraid that he would be lost after he had been saved and serving!

"This erroneous idea would never have been rooted, if we had possessed the knowledge, when the New Testament was rendered into the English, that has since come to us from archeology. The whole matter turns on the meaning of the word Paul uses here, ADOKIMOS. This Koine word was lost to the world for ages, and is just recovered from the ostraca. It was a common household word in the days of Paul, and was applied to a certain pottery

vessel in sad condition. Remembering that all the
utensils of household service were pottery, it is easy
to understand how often such would be cracked or
broken. A woman, busy about the hearthstone with
a pottery cooking vessel in her hand, in careless
haste might bump the pot against the stones and
crack it so that it would no longer hold water.

"Did she then throw away this leaky vessel? You
know she did not! Just step to your own pantry and
see how many tea cups there are on that shelf, with
a handle broken off, or an unsightly crack marring
the smooth surface of the porcelain! Never forget
that we are dealing with FOLKS in these old dis-
coveries, and that human nature has not changed
one iota in two thousand years! So the ancient house-
keeper, having a cracked pot that was no longer fit
for boiling water, PUT IT ON THE SHELF. Perhaps she hoped to use it again as a receptacle for
beans or wheat, perhaps she was just thrifty; but
when a pot was cracked and laid on the shelf, it was
called ADOKIMOS! Was it Lost? No! It was just
laid aside.

"So Paul, contemplating the effects of sin in the
Christian life, states in terms that his readers could
most appreciate, 'I strive so to live that I may not be
PUT ON THE SHELF!' To how many living men
would that phrase be aptly applied! Do we not all of
us know men who have been used of God in His
service, who allowed the flesh to gain the ascend-
ancy? Where are those men today? In the language
of Paul, which is strangely reminiscent of the slang
of this age, 'they are on the shelf.' So Paul writes of

his ministry, and says, 'I do not want to be a cracked pot! (Adokimos).' "

In Philippians 3:11 Paul says, "If by any means I might attain unto the resurrection of the dead." This is made to teach that Paul could have been lost, because his participation in that resurrection which takes place when Christ comes for His Church was dependent upon his present striving as indicated in the preceding verses.

So to interpret this passage is not only to compromise grace principles, but it completely denies that salvation is by grace and that eternal life is a gift of God.

This passage can not possibly refer to the resurrection of the body. In the next verse Paul says that he has not yet attained thereto. It would be meaningless for one not yet dead to say that he had not been raised from the grave. The resurrection to which Paul refers must be something attainable in the earthly life of the believer.

The following interpretation is offered, not only as in perfect harmony with the doctrines of the grace of God, but also as suggested by other Scripture passages.

In this verse and the preceding one the fellowship of the sufferings of Christ and the conformability unto His death are related to the resurrection of the dead. In 2 Corinthians 4:10, and 11 are also found, though in different words, the same two conditions, the fellowship of suffering and conformity unto the death of Christ. There it is clearly stated that the purpose of these two is that the life of Christ might be made manifest in the mortal (subject to death) body. This then suggests that the resurrection of Philippians 3:11 is the same as the manifestation of the life of Christ in the present mortal body of the believer. This suggestion is strongly supported by Romans 6:4, wherein the new life of the believer is likened unto Christ's resurrection from the dead.

Furthermore the words, "Not as though I had already attained, either were already perfect," (Phil. 3:12) seem to support even further the suggestion that "the resurrection of the dead" means the full manifestation of the life of Christ in the present mortal body. Surely here is life out of death.

1 John 5:16 is sufficient grounds for some to deny the eternal security of the believer. It reads: "If any man see his brother sin a sin which is not unto death, he shall ask, and he shall give him life for them that sin not unto death. There is a sin unto death: I do not say that he shall pray for it." The meaning of this verse depends upon the meaning of the words death and life. They are said to mean eternal life and everlasting death or condemnation. *No other Scripture passage is ever quoted to support the interpretation.* This interpretation is fraught with at least five distinct errors:

1. It flatly contradicts the words of Jesus (also recorded by John): "He that . . . believeth . . . hath everlasting life, and shall not come into condemnation" (John 5:24).

2. It denies the intercessory work of Christ (also recorded by John and in the same epistle): "If any man sin, we have an Advocate with the Father, Jesus

Christ the Righteous, and He is the propitiation for our sins."

3. To teach that one man can pray for another and thereby the one prayed for is delivered from the guilt of his sin and given eternal life is to recognize a human mediatorship between God and man as the Roman Church does. This is contrary to God's own Word: "There is . . . One Mediator between God and man, the Man Christ Jesus" (1 Tim. 2:5).

4. It classifies sin (in the sense of transgression of the law) into two classes; those capable of being forgiven and those that take away grace and involve the death of the soul. These are the venial and mortal sins of Roman theology, pure and simple. In relation to eternal life or everlasting death, there are no degrees of sin, all are the same. James writes (Jas. 2:10): "For whosoever shall keep the whole law, and yet offend in one point, he is guilty of all."

5. It teaches that through the prayer of another, a *believer* secures forgiveness of sin. This cannot be supported by other Scripture passages. In fact it is contradicted by a passage which also is recorded by John and in the same letter: "If *we* confess *our* sins, He is faithful and just to forgive us our sins, and cleanse us from all unrighteousness" (1 John 1:9). It is one's own confession, not the prayer of another, which God honors in forgiving a sinning saint.

This illustrates the awful error into which it is possible to fall when an individual passage is interpreted apart from the great fundamental doctrines of the Bible.

There is another interpretation of this passage that

can be supported by other passages and does not do violence to any of the great doctrines of the Bible. This interpretation considers the word "death" to mean physical death. That physical death can result from sin is clearly taught in 1 Corinthians 11:29, 30 R. V. "For he that eateth and drinketh [the Lord's supper], eateth and drinketh judgment unto himself, if he discern not the body. For this cause many among you are weak and sickly, and not a few sleep." The word "sleep" is used of the physical death of believers. Jesus said that Lazarus slept when he was dead (John 11:11). When stoned, Stephen "fell asleep" (Acts 7:60).

Thus there were those in the Corinthian church who had died the physical death because of sin, but they were not lost because the word "sleep" is never used for death except in the case of those who are saved. It is, therefore, in perfect accord with the clear teaching of the Bible to interpret the word death as meaning physical death. Thus it seems most reasonable in the light of other Scripture to interpret the passage in question as an injunction to pray for persons who are sick because of sins committed that they may be restored to health, yet in the case of some sin, prayer shall not be offered. This interpretation must not of course be made to support the false teaching that all sickness is due to sins committed by the sick person.

28

Misinterpreted Bible Passages—Continued

A SERIOUS ERROR committed by those who deny eternal security is to use passages that are in figurative language to prove the contention that one who has been saved can be lost. It is only after a given interpretation of a figurative passage has been fully authenticated by other Scripture that it can be used as proof. To use interpretations not so authenticated *is to base doctrine on purely human thinking and reasoning.* Doctrine, which is truth, in order to be true must be a divine revelation.

A SOWER WENT OUT TO SOW

The parable of the sower (Matt. 13:1-23) is an outstanding example of this class of passages. It is claimed that the seed that grows in the stony ground and among thorns represents persons that are saved, but who became backsliders and are lost. This interpretation is never sustained by other Scripture passages. In the first place, such interpretation directly denies salvation by grace through faith and all the other doctrines considered in Chapters V-XVII and therefore must be dismissed.

There is a key word in this parable, the significance of which is learned from several passages. That word is "fruit." There were two kinds of growth, that which bore no fruit and that which bore fruit. In connection with the first use of the word fruit (Gen. 1:11), it is said that it contains the seed. Therefore, according to the law of first mention where there is fruit, there is seed and where there is no fruit, there is no seed. That which grew among the rocks and the thorns, bore no fruit hence it had no seed in it, while that which bore fruit did have seed. As has previously been mentioned, all who are born again (i. e., saved) are born "of incorruptible seed by the Word of God" (1 Pet. 1:23), and that seed remains in them (1 John 3:9). Thus the Bible clearly makes the continuing presence of seed a sign of new birth. The absence thereof becomes a sign that regeneration has not taken place. Natural man and all the moral development and the so-called Christian culture, apart from regeneration, is flesh which is as the grass and the flower thereof that withers. Jesus speaking of Himself said: "Except a corn of wheat fall into the ground and die it abideth alone; but if it die, it *bringeth forth much fruit*." This "much fruit" are those who are saved through His death and resurrection. Note carefully, they are "fruit"—not the blade and the stalk which withers.

The life that is in the seed of any grain today is the same life as was in the seed, of that same kind of grain, that God made and put into the earth on the third creation day. Therefore, seed means the enduring life and stands for the eternal life of a saved person; whereas the stalk which has a life of a very limited duration, represents flesh or the earthly life of man.

It is very interesting to notice that to the perfect creation before the fall, God gave to the beast "every *green* herb"; but to man He gave "every herb *bearing seed*" and "every tree, in the which is the *fruit* of a tree *yielding seed.*" Here seed undoubtedly stands for spiritual food, whereas herbs represent mere bodily food. In the light of these different passages, harmonizing with each other, it seems only reasonable to conclude that only that which bore fruit represents saved men and women. That which bore no fruit represents merely natural men who have either been stirred emotionally with outward signs similar to spiritual manifestations or who have only been morally improved due to hearing the teachings of the Word. That the Word of God is a great influence for human uplift, even in the lives of persons that are not born again, cannot be denied. Considerable space has been given to this passage not only because of its importance, but also because the same issue arises in the next passage for consideration.

THE VINE AND THE BRANCHES

In John 15:1-6 is the record of the words of Jesus concerning the Vine and the branches. This passage is a particularly favorite one of those who claim that one who has been saved can be lost. It is said that every branch in Jesus is a saved person and the branches that are cut off are saved persons who are lost.

Much can be said to refute this interpretation. All agree that there are two kinds of branches; those not bearing fruit and those bearing fruit. It has already been shown at some length in the discussion of the previous passage that fruit and seed are a sign of being born again. As the unfruitful branches do not have this sign, it is only reasonable to conclude that they cannot represent saved persons.

On the other hand, the fruitful branches have seed and are children of God. But the Father Husbandman cares for these branches in a special way—He purges them. He removes part of the woody growth so that they will bear more fruit. This is exactly what the "Father" does with every one that is born of incorruptible seed—everyone who is His child.

"The Lord scourgeth *every* son whom He receiveth" and, "if ye be without chastening [R. V.] whereof *all* are partakers, then are ye bastards, and not sons" (Heb. 12:6, 8). And significantly enough, the purpose of this chastening is exactly the same as the purging of the fruitful branches, to bear more fruit in the form of righteousness (Heb. 12:11).

The unfruitful branches are not purged. Thus in a twofold way, the two kinds of branches are identified by other Scripture passages. The unfruitful branches cannot be saved persons, because they definitely lack the two indispensable signs of sonship, having seed in them and being chastened.

It is still contended that the expression, "in Me," can only mean a saved person for, "if any man be in Christ, he is a new creature" (2 Cor. 5:17). This would be true if the words "in me" had the same meaning as "in Christ," but there is much to show that they do not. The message of the Gospel of

John is "the Word was made flesh"—the Son of God becomes the Son of man and in Him is life—life both in a universal sense for all men, and in an individual sense only for those who believe.

It was as the Son of man that He became identified with the whole human race. He said, "And I, if I be lifted up from the earth, will draw *all* men unto Me" (John 12:32). That He said this of Himself as the Son of man is clear from the immediately preceding statement, "The hour is come that the Son of man should be glorified" (v. 23) and an earlier statement, "As Moses lifted up the serpent in the wilderness, even so must the Son of man be lifted up" (John 3:14).

By this drawing of "all men unto" Himself, life passed from Him unto *all* men. Death entered the human race by sin (Rom. 5:12). On the cross the Son of man took away all sin, for He was "the Lamb of God which taketh away the sin of the world" (John 1:29). Thus that by which death entered the human race (Rom. 5:12) was removed, and life was brought back to the human race. That He gave life to all is clearly taught in John 6:33: "For the bread of God is He which cometh down from Heaven and giveth life unto the world." "In Him was life; and the life was the light of men." "That was the true Light, which lighteth *every man* that cometh into the world" (John 1:4, 9).

There is still another statement as to life in the Son of man that applies to all men. "Marvel not at this: for the hour is coming, in which *all* that are in the graves shall hear His [the Son of man's] voice and shall come forth; they that have done good unto the resurrection of life; and they that have done evil, unto the resurrection of damnation" (John 5:29). This is the bodily resurrection of all men which was made possible only by the death and resurrection of the Son of man. "For since by *man* came death, by *man* [the Son of man] came also the resurrection of the dead" (1 Cor. 15:21). Thus in Him Who said, "every branch *in Me*," there is life in a universal sense. It is for *all* men. This life is on a purely human plane. It is not divine, nor is it eternal. In the figure, it is represented by the corruptible wood and leaves of the branches.

"In Him" there is also a divine life that becomes *available* to all because of the fact that He has overcome for all, that physical death which came through Adam's sin. He, on the cross, became, in His humanity, united with all men. Those who through faith in Him as the Son of God become united with Him in His divine being are become children of God. They are "in Christ" and have eternal life.

As the gospel of John clearly teaches the universality of life, of a human nature, in the Son of man, so it also teaches the certainty of a divine eternal life in the Son of God for a limited number—all who believe. While He drew *all* men unto Himself on the cross, only those who receive Him are born of God (John 1:12, 13) and those who believe on Him as the only begotten Son of God have eternal life (John 3:16). He was the bread of God from heaven that "giveth life unto the world, but only those who eat His flesh and drink His blood have *eternal life*" (John 6:33, 54).

Thus Jesus (as recorded by John) taught that there was life in Him in this twofold sense. He also made it clear that for some the resurrection of the body was unto life, while for others it was unto damnation (John 5:29). In other words, some are raised unto life which is a continued union with Him while others are raised to life for the purpose of condemnation, that is separation from Him. And is not this in perfect harmony with what happens to the branches? Some are separated and some continue in union with Him.

Thus this word picture of the Vine and the branches, with corruptible wood representing humanity, and fruit with its seed, divine life, is a perfect and full illustration of what He Who was both Son of man and Son of God accomplished for the human race. He spoke this Himself at the very moment that He faced the cross by which all was brought to pass. What harmony there is in it all! Contrast this with that school of interpretation of Scripture which never hesitates to make some difficult passage contradict the, "Verily, verily, I say unto you" (John 5:24) of the Son of God.

Much more can be said about this passage, but this is not an exposition of it, except insofar as it is used to deny the eternal security of every saved person.

There are, however, two other verses in this passage that are made to deny eternal security. The words, "Abide in Me and I in you" and "Except ye abide in Me" are offered as a proof that one who is in Christ can be separated from Him. As the words "abide in Me and I in you," are addressed to such as have been declared to be clean (v. 3), they must be applied to saved persons only and not to saved and unsaved as in verse two. Here is a definite command by God and the reason for it follows; but it is not an obligation placed on the saved one, as is clear from the last three words. A comparable command is found in Luke 5:13. Jesus there said to the man full of leprosy, "Be thou clean." This clearly does not imply that the man was to cleanse himself. So also the command, "Abide in Me and I in you," does not mean that those who have been cleansed by a similar command on His part must keep themselves in Him. The Lord's command to the sinner to be clean and to the cleansed one to abide are both brought to realization by His own power. This command then states the law of divine life in Him as being a continuous need on the part of the one who has been washed by *the* washing of regeneration, to remain in continuous union with Him. From His own words (recorded in the same gospel), "He that believeth . . . hath *everlasting* life [eternal union with Him] and shall not come into condemnation [separation from Him]," it is clear that His command cannot be broken. It can just as truly be said that unless the sun and the earth remain in their orbits, day will not follow night and Spring will not follow Winter as to say, "No more can ye [bear fruit] except ye abide in Me." No one would say that the sun and the earth must by their own power remain in their orbits. No. They are kept there by the Creator's power. And so is every saved person kept in Christ by the power of God.

The sixth verse is also used to prove that a saved person can be lost. Those who use it so overlook the statement that those spoken of are gathered and cast into the fire by *men*. To be lost is to be cast out *by God,* as in the second verse. Anything which is said to be done by *men* cannot by any stretch of the imagination be interpreted as meaning condemnation.

This same error is made by those who misinterpret Matthew 5:13, as teaching that a saved person can be lost. When the salt has lost its savor, it is trodden under foot of *men*. These verses deal only with an earthly condition and have nothing to say as to the eternal state. The purpose of this passage as applied to believers is to warn them that their influence for God among the unsaved can be lost, but not that they will lose their eternal life.

The parable of the Ten Virgins (Matt. 25:1-13) is another favorite passage used by those who deny eternal security to prove their contention. There are probably more different interpretations given this passage than any other. To make such a passage contradict the clear teaching of the doctrines of the grace of God is to explain the known by the unknown. It is to interpret the clear by the vague and the result can be nothing but confusion. The very fact, that a disputed passage as this is used to deny the eternal security of the believer is a confession of weakness on the part of those who so use it.

Additional misinterpreted passages that are quoted to prove that one who has been saved can be lost, might be quoted at considerable length, but space does not permit, nor is it necessary. Those quoted ought to be sufficient to point out that the purported scriptural support for the denial of eternal security consists only in misinterpretations of Bible passages. These interpretations deny the plain, fundamental truth of God's Word. *True Bible exposition demands that obscure and difficult passages be carefully studied in the light of plain teachings.*

To misinterpret God's Word is a wile of Satan that started in the Garden and caused the first Adam to sin and become the head of a sinful race. He used it also, though unsuccessfully, when he was permitted to tempt the Son of man, the last Adam. Though he cannot rob them of their eternal life, he does it today to rob God's children of their assurance which brings peace and joy and a fruitful life for God. And he does this through men who are innocent of his workings.

If anyone who still rejects this precious truth feels that an insufficient number of difficult passages have been explained, let him go back and first harmonize his own position with the great doctrines of the grace of God as explained in Chapter V to XVII. When that has been done, it is time to seek explanations for any remaining difficult passages. In fact, many difficulties will then of themselves have disappeared, just as do the difficulties of the infidel, when he is willing to accept the essential truth concerning God and His Christ.

29
A Veil Over the Understanding

IN DISCUSSING the evils of Arminianism in this and the following three chapters, the term is used in its popular sense which restricts it to the single doctrine that "man may relapse from a state of grace"; that is, one who has been saved may be lost. That is the only tenet of that system of theology with which this discussion is concerned.

In this criticism of Arminianism, it is not the individuals themselves who reject eternal security, to a greater or less degree, who are being considered. With many of them, their rejection is largely a matter of terminology. With others it is a lack of knowledge, for which they themselves can hardly be held responsible because they have never been taught. *The criticism here is directed at the teaching itself.*

Furthermore, what is here said must not be construed as meaning that the good which has been accomplished by sincere and consecrated men and women has no value because of their views on this question. Nothing that follows must be taken to minimize in any way the work done for the Lord by many who do not hold the views presented here.

It can be granted freely that there have been Arminian Christians who have accomplished more for God's Kingdom than some Calvinistic Christians, without refuting the statements made in these four chapters. *The question is: what is the influence of the teaching that one who has been saved can be lost, upon those who are being taught?*

Throughout the foregoing pages, references have been made to evils resulting from the Arminian teaching. In order that the full significance of these might be realized, even at the danger of repetition, these are brought together and additional ones are mentioned in this section.

The teaching that a person who has been saved can be lost casts a veil over the understanding in the reading of the great doctrinal epistles. More than one person will testify that the Pauline letters could not be understood by them as long as they did not accept the doctrine of eternal security. Why this is so can be made clear by a simple illustration.

BLEEDING THROUGH

Everyone familiar with painting knows how difficult it is to cover with some other color that which has been painted red. The red always, in the words of the painter, "bleeds through." Even the red in brown paint will bleed through and change any color that is painted over it. So also is it with the teaching that one who has been saved can be lost. To illustrate: There are many who say that they believe that a person is saved by grace. But what do they mean? Certainly something vastly different than explained in Chapter VI. To them, to be saved by grace means to have all sins committed up to that moment, forgiven. The saved one is placed in a position so that if he maintains the proper conduct (whatever that might be), he will receive eternal life when the earthly life's journey is ended. They do not put it that clearly, but that is a perfectly fair statement of their position. The requirements to maintain the state of grace vary. One man said most emphatically, "One is saved by grace, but one must keep the Sabbath." With others the "musts" are quite different, but it is exactly the same principle. The saved one must do something, be it this or that, or he will be lost.

This notion that a saved person can be lost, bleeds through the statement: "wherefore He is able also to save them to the uttermost that come unto God by Him, seeing He ever liveth to make intercession for them" (Heb. 7:25) and makes this passage mean that Christ is able to save from the lowest depths of sin. The beautiful shade of meaning intended in this verse is the continuing salvation because, "He ever liveth." God's color scheme is therefore entirely destroyed.

One man who for years had listened to Arminian preaching discovered that man is not justified by the works of the law. But instead of seeing that it was of grace alone through faith, he came to the conclusion that the one who has been saved by grace is justified by the *works of faith* which he does. This was nothing but the "bleeding through" of the notion that a Christian would be lost if he did not maintain good works.

And so all of the doctrines of grace are bled through so much so that they lose their beautiful color that God has given them.

There is a veil cast over the understanding so that the doctrines of grace, as revealed in Paul's writings, are not understood. They cannot be understood until the veil be removed. But when it has been removed, in what glorious splendor do not these doctrines shine!

CANNOT BELIEVE

But the evil goes even farther than to hinder the understanding: it even becomes *impossible to believe*. In Chapter X was related the story of one who, on being told that eternal life is a present possession of every believer, said: "I *can't believe* that we now have eternal life, for that would be eternal security and I won't believe that." It is sadly true that rejection of the doctrine of eternal security actually makes it *impossible* for some to believe the doctrines of grace.

CAUSES CONFUSED TEACHING

The interpretation of the Bible from the Arminian viewpoint leads to confusion rather than clarity. By interpreting warnings against the loss of rewards as meaning the possible loss of eternal life, the two entirely separate subjects of eternal life and rewards are sadly confused. In the same way, what God's Word teaches about those who are mere professors of Christianity is confused as applying to true believers. By applying Old Testament teachings and passages of a purely legal nature to saved persons of this age, law and grace become hopelessly mixed in the thinking of vast numbers of Christians. As Paul places much emphasis upon the fact that believers are *"not under the law, but under grace"* (Rom. 6:14), this confused teaching is decidedly harmful.

People ask, "Why is the Bible written in such a way that it is so hard to understand?" The difficulty is not with the Bible, but with much teaching that causes the Bible to seem to be confused. The mistaken idea that man must do something meritorious in order to enter into heaven, which is inherent in the Arminian teaching, is responsible for many of the difficulties which are a hindrance to a clear understanding of the Bible.

INCONSISTENT POSITIONS

Those who reject eternal security often place themselves in inconsistent positions.

A minister who, to a considerable extent, in his public utterances has denounced eternal security, made the following statement in a sermon: "God saved me and God keeps me. I don't know which is the more important." By considering God's keeping work equal to His saving work, he either admitted his own eternal security or otherwise he questioned his own salvation. It is reasonable to assume that he did not question his salvation. If so, then he contradicted all his attacks on eternal security.

It is not uncommon for an unsaved person who is being entreated to "become saved" to answer, "I would like to be a Christian but I feel I cannot hold out." To this many an Arminian has replied, "*God will keep you.*" Honestly, do they really mean that? If so, how then can they deny eternal security? To press this matter just a little further, why does the unsaved man make such a statement as he does? There is just one reason for it—the Arminian teaching that one who has been saved can be lost. The teaching of those who are entreating him to become saved has created a state of mind in the unsaved which hinders the acceptance of the Gospel.

It is true that many who reject the doctrine of eternal security are absolutely certain of their own eternal state. They are certain that they shall not be lost. How inconsistent! Has God made a special provision for them? Has the blood of Christ greater efficacy for them than for others? Or does Christ, the Advocate, plead their case better than that of someone else? Possibly they have a stronger character than the weaker brother who might be lost because he is addicted to drink or some other habit? Possibly the last is the thought that is unconsciously lurking in their minds. But then salvation would be of works, and God says it is not.

If it is possible for one to become lost, the same possibility exists for every saved person. To feel secure as to oneself, and by one's teaching rob others of their assurance is worse than being inconsistent.

Thus the Arminian teaching that one who has been saved can be lost, casts a veil over the doctrines of grace so that they cannot be fully understood; in fact, at times cannot be believed. It also causes a confused presentation of the Gospel of the grace of God and often places its adherents in inconsistent positions. If this were all that could be said against this doctrine, it would be enough to condemn it, but there is more.

30

It Causes Spiritual Depression

"OR IF the trumpet give an uncertain sound, who shall prepare himself to the battle?" (1 Cor. 14:8). If this challenge be true, and it is true, then what effect will the uncertain Arminian message that is both yea and nay have upon those to whom it is given? What type of Christian life can be expected from it?

The very possibility of being *lost* causes uncertainty as to eternity.

The basic cause of the unprecedented economic depression of the last few years is lack of confidence, or uncertainty as to the future. Men do not invest money in enterprises from which returns are questionable. So also in spiritual matters uncertainty causes a depression in the level of Christian living.

IT ROBS BELIEVERS OF ASSURANCE

This uncertainty as to eternity first of all robs the believer of his assurance. There seem to be those who go through life without ever a moment of enjoyment of the anticipated glory that lies ahead. This is so because they are not certain that they shall ever reach that glory. With others, the periods of doubt and questioning are broken by flashes of hope and joy at special occasions.

184

The thought of the Lord's return, instead of being a blessed hope that brings joy and peace into the soul, becomes the cause of fear and trembling that one might be left.

With some there seem to be times in their lives, especially during periods of revival, when there is no question whatsoever about their security. The promises of God are accepted without reservation. But when the enthusiasm and emotions of the revival are over and temptations come, when mistakes have been made, then the assurance is gone. There is nothing left to carry them through the times of testing.

SELF-CENTERED INSTEAD OF CHRIST-CENTERED

When Christians are told that they might be lost, it is often as a warning to desist from something they are doing, or to do that which is being neglected. That type of preaching centers the believer's thoughts upon himself. He begins to look into his life and compares it with the lives of others. He sees his failures and checks them with what he has wrongly been told is God's requirement for entrance into glory. The more honest he is, the more despondent he becomes, and it does not take long before he dares not say that he is saved. This is not theory. It has been the sad experience of altogether too many young people within churches condoning the Arminian doctrine.

All of the believer's hope for eternity is centered in the perfection of Christ and in His finished work.

But whatever might be said of that fact is largely lost by the repeated warnings that one might be lost.

Assurance, which is greatly lacking in many groups, is indispensable to a consistent, happy and fruitful Christian life.

FEAR AS DYNAMIC FOR GODLY LIFE

One who for years has attended a church that holds the Arminian view, once said, "It seems that our preachers think that they must frighten us into being good." That man struck at the very heart of one of the great evils of Arminian teaching. To threaten Christians with the possibility of their being lost in order to arouse them from spiritual lethargy is directly opposite to Paul's—"The love of Christ constraineth us."

There is a real place for the fear of God in the life of a Christian, but that is *filial* fear and not that servile fear which results from threats of condemnation.

Servile fear of God leads to attempts at self-justification. And so the attempt to arouse from spiritual lethargy by the principle of fear leads to a struggle to accomplish by one's own meritorious acts that which Christ has already done.

Fear tears down, it destroys that which is. It sends no man into battle. It is a hindrance, not a help. And it has no place in the Christian life: "For ye have not received the spirit of bondage again to fear; but ye have received the Spirit of adoption, whereby we cry Abba, Father" (Rom. 8:15). "For God hath not given us the spirit of fear; but of power, and of love; and of a sound mind" (2 Tim. 1:7).

Love, not fear, is the true motive of the Christian life. These two are contrary, the one to the other. "There is no fear in love; but perfect love casteth out fear: because fear hath torment. He that feareth is not made perfect in love" (1 John 4:18).

How terrible it is then to teach the possible loss of eternal life and instill fear in the lives of believers. It causes untold torment and keeps persons from becoming perfect in love.

DESTROYS REST THAT COMES FROM TRUST IN GOD

No Christian who is in fear of being lost can rest in the promises of God. There is a constant struggling in self-effort to keep oneself saved. Such cannot realize the meaning of Hebrews 4:10, "For he that hath entered into His rest, he also hath ceased from his own works, as God did from His."

WEAKENS FAITH

As has previously been pointed out (p. 141), it is through lack of faith that the Christian fails to enter into rest. Lack of faith also hinders and even interferes with the Lord's work. Therefore that which weakens or destroys faith is clearly a hindrance to the furtherance of the Kingdom of God.

To magnify the object of a person's faith is to increase his faith in that object, but to detract from the value of such an object is to lessen faith in it. Therefore, to magnify the work of the Triune God in salvation, strengthens the believer's faith; but to minimize it weakens his faith. To teach that one who has been saved through the operation of the grace of God can be lost, is to minimize His work. Either God is not able to finish what He has begun, as is implied in the argument of the free moral agency of man, or He does not hold Himself responsible to do so. Whatever view one might wish to take, it certainly discounts God. He is either not omnipotent, or He ceases to love and exercise grace. Thus God becomes finite instead of infinite. The one who teaches eternal security points to an omnipotent God Who loves with an everlasting love, and Whose grace is sovereign. Those who reject eternal security may contend that they believe in an infinite God, but their arguments do not bear this out. See the next chapter for more on this subject. Thus, by limiting God, the Arminian position weakens the faith of the believer.

But that is not all. Only as an object attracts attention can it inspire faith. By constantly speaking of the believer's condition, whether it be the sufficiency of his faith or his conduct, attention is centered in the believer instead of in God. Faith is thereby still further weakened. Certainly the Arminian teaching does not help to strengthen faith in God and His Son and the finished Work on Calvary.

IT CAUSES CARELESS CHRISTIAN LIVING

In the third section of this book, it was shown that the denial of the truth of eternal security discounts the mercies of God upon which He bases His appeal for a godly life and therefore the Arminian position causes carelessness in Christian living. But that is not all that can be said to place responsibility for low Christian standards of life upon those that contend for that position.

There is a teaching which seems to go hand in hand with the denial of eternal security. This can be stated as follows: our God is gracious and long-suffering and will overlook our failures and shortcomings. Let the reader judge for himself. Which is the most conducive to careless Christian living: this teaching that small sins are overlooked by God, or the teaching upon which eternal security rests, that Christ suffered and died on Calvary's cross as a propitiation for even the smallest sin committed by a believer?

It is here charged then that Arminianism by teaching uncertainty as to eternity causes spiritual depression. It robs believers of assurance; tends to make Christians self-centered instead of Christ-centered. It makes fear the dynamic of godly life instead of love. It destroys the rest and peace that come from trusting in the finished work of Christ. It weakens faith and is conducive to careless Christian living.

31

Denies the Infiniteness of the Word, Work and Nature of God

H E [GOD] only is my Rock and my Salvation" (Psa. 62:2). The one who accepts eternal security accepts this statement at its face value, but Arminianism does not. It teaches: "Salvation is of God and myself." This is the fundamental difference between the two positions. Many a person who rejects the truth of eternal security will deny this statement, but the arguments that are presented to support the Arminian position conclusively prove that this is true.

No argument has yet been offered to prove that a saved person can be lost, which is not based on some human element. It is said, *man can will* to go away from God; *man can cease* to believe; *man can* willfully sin and be lost; if a saved *man does* not confess his sins, he is lost; *man must* remain in Christ; et cetera. *What are these but human increments which are added in order to guarantee salvation? Surely it is nothing other than, "Salvation is by God and man."*

To insist upon this human increment in order to remain saved, is to teach that God cannot save without the assistance of man. Thus God is limited in relation to man's salvation. Salvation, as far as has

190

been revealed to man, is the greatest work that God has undertaken. If He is limited in this, His work is not infinite, nor is He Himself infinite.

The purpose of this chapter is to show that the Arminian position denies that God is infinite. Arminians will deny that this is so, but the proof of the statement lies in comparing their arguments with God's Word.

GOD'S WORD MADE FINITE

If the possibility of a *single* saved person being lost is granted, then the following statements and others from God's Word, as quoted in Chapter IV, are not absolute; they have only a relative meaning and therefore they are finite. "All that the Father giveth Me shall come unto Me." "I give them [My sheep] eternal life." "My sheep . . . shall never perish." "There is therefore now no condemnation to them that are in Christ Jesus." "God shall deliver me from every evil work, and will preserve me unto His heavenly Kingdom." These statements are all made concerning those who are saved. Everyone of them is being limited by the human (finite) interpretations of the Arminian teachings and thus is made to partake of a finite nature.

GOD'S WORK IS MADE FINITE

In the doctrines of the grace of God is revealed that which He has accomplished through Christ in behalf of every saved person. *If the work that God has done is infinite, then there can be no failure; but if there is possibility of failure, then the work cannot be infinite.* To contend that one who has been saved can be lost, is to say that there is possibility of failure, and this in turn, is nothing less than to deny the absolute and infinite nature of God's work in saving man.

This may be seen more clearly by considering separately some of those things which God has done.

In the first place, before God can work on the principle of grace, it is necessary that there be no merit in man. There can be no place whatsoever for human boasting. This is made clear in God's Word. It is "not of works, lest any man should boast" (Eph. 2:9). And again, "Where is boasting then? It is excluded. By what law? of works? Nay: but by the law of faith" (Rom. 3:27). God's program excludes all human boasting. No flesh shall glory in His presence (1 Cor. 1:29).

But the Arminian view, by insisting on introducing a human element into man's salvation, denies this position of absolute worthlessness on the part of man. With them there is something in man that has value, and consequently there is human boasting. Thus God's fundamental requirement to act in grace is not absolute. If that be granted, it is impossible for God's work to be infinite; because what He would then do is but to add to what is already in man. However minute a particle of merit is conceded to be in man, it is sufficient to keep God's work of salvation from being infinite.

By denying the absolute depravity of man, the absoluteness of grace is also denied, for grace cannot operate where there is human merit. "And if by grace, then it is no more of works: otherwise grace is no more grace. But if it be of works, then it is no more grace: otherwise work is no more work" (Rom. 11:6). Thus the grace of God by which man is saved becomes finite.

Again, the argument that man is a free moral agent and can go away from God limits grace and very definitely reduces the grace of God from being of an infinite nature to a finite thing.

The calling of God unto the obtaining of the Glory of Jesus Christ (2 Thess. 2:14) becomes a limited calling, if it is possible for one who has been called to come short of obtaining that Glory. It too becomes finite instead of infinite.

The gifts of God—His Son, eternal life, righteousness and the Holy Spirit—are not gifts in the absolute sense of the word, if it is possible to lose them through failure to comply with some requirement as the Arminians teach. According to man's finite thinking, things are called gifts which would never have been given had not something else previously been given. Man "exchanges" gifts with his fellow man. But with God a gift is so in an unqualified sense. To teach otherwise is to make God's gifts finite instead of infinite.

If one who has been saved by the substitutionary death of Christ, can be lost, then the death of Christ does not have unlimited value. There must be something that in some way neutralizes its value. Then the statement that He hath appeared to "put away sin by the sacrifice of Himself" (Heb. 9:26) does not have infinite value for everyone who bases his hope of glory on that sacrifice.

Redemption is only finite if one who has been redeemed can again be placed in a position of condemnation under the law. Then also, the blood of Christ which is the redemption price does not have infinite value. The Arminian teaching thus denies the infinite value of the blood of Christ as a propitiation for sin.

As justification is through the redemption that is in Christ Jesus (Rom. 3:24), it also loses its infinite character if redemption is not of an infinite nature.

The eternal life given through the new birth, the regeneration by the incorruptible Word of God, is not infinite if it can die. (See Chapter X.)

If one who has been saved and is of the new creation in Christ Jesus can be lost, then that creation is subject to death and therefore cannot be infinite in its nature.

And finally the Arminian position does not allow absolute glory to God, for if the human element be recognized in salvation then all the glory does not belong to Him. He cannot accept glory for that which He has not done.

The Arminian teaching is most inconsistent with that scene pictured in Revelation of infinite honor and glory being given to Him "that sitteth upon the throne" (Rev. 4:9-11 and 5:9-13).

Thus by insisting upon a human element in salvation, Arminianism not only attacks the absoluteness of God's Word, but also denies the infinite nature of His work of grace in salvation.

THE INFINITE NATURE OF GOD IS QUESTIONED

But the implications from their arguments are even more serious if that is possible. These attack the very character and nature of God Himself.

Jesus prayed, "Holy Father, keep through Thine own Name those whom Thou hast given Me" (John 17:11). That this is in behalf of all believers is made perfectly clear by His words uttered later on in the same prayer: "Neither pray I for these alone, but for them also which shall believe on Me through their word" (v. 20). In this prayer, then, Jesus asks the Father to keep in His own Name all who are saved through believing on Him. *If a single saved person becomes lost, this prayer is not fully answered.* Therefore the Arminian, by saying that some are lost, says that the Father does not completely answer the prayer of the Son. Such a condition would demand either that the Father is unable to answer it or that the Son has not met the requirements of the Father in order to receive an answer. If the Father cannot answer, He is not omnipotent and consequently He is not infinite. If the Son has not met some condition necessary to receive answer to His prayer, then He is not fully in the will of the Father. If not fully in the will of the Father, He is not absolutely righteous and consequently not infinite.

Thus the very nature of the Godhead is assailed

by the argument that one who has been saved can be lost. Both His righteousness and His omnipotence are questioned, and either one or the other is denied.

The teaching mentioned in the preceding chapter, that God is gracious and long-suffering and will overlook our failures and shortcomings, denies the absolute righteousness and justice of God. Called by their Bible name, shortcomings and failures are sins. God's holy law demands the death penalty for sin. For God to overlook a single sin would be for Him to compromise His own righteousness and justice. To contend that there is one compromise is to say that He is finite. Thus God cannot be infinite in His righteousness and justice and do as so many Arminians teach that He does.

In Chapter XII, p. 56, it was shown that the omniscience of God is called into question by rejecting the truth of eternal security. Thus, in still another of His attributes, is the infiniteness of God questioned.

It has been shown (Chapter XV) that God loves those who are His own with an everlasting love. If one who has become His very own should by sinning be lost, then the eternal love would cease and be replaced by wrath. Then God's love could be limited by an act of finite man and would not be infinite.

Thus the infinite nature of God, by virtue of which He is God, is denied. This is all done by adding the human increment as necessary to that salvation, which God claims is entirely of Himself.

It must be apparent from this, that there is no room even for the position: "It is not probable that a saved person will be lost, but there is a possibility." If a *single one* can be lost, then God in all of these attributes that have been mentioned is not infinite—there is some limitation. If it were but one out of a billion it would be sufficient to destroy the infinite nature of God's work in saving men.

There are many who contend for the infinite nature of God, of His works and of His Word, who teach that a saved person can be lost. This, however, does not alter the claim that is here made, that the teaching that a saved person can be lost attacks the very nature of God, of His Works and of His Word.

32

Arminianism and Modernism

IT HAS already been stated that not a single argument is offered against eternal security, but what is based upon some human element as necessary to salvation. Often this is in so subtle a manner and to such a small degree that it is not so recognized. None the less the human element is present. The arguments for eternal security are based on the sufficiency of God and His work to the exclusion of every particle of the human element. *The difference is of tremendous importance, for the Arminian arguments establish the principle that man must contribute to his salvation from the penalty of sin. The gulf between these two is nothing less than the gulf that exists between the divine and the human, the infinite and the finite.*

After the principle has once been established, it is only a matter of degrees to add more and more of the human, a little at a time, and require less and less of the divine. By this process Modernism is soon reached. The next step is Humanism, which rules God out entirely—man is sufficient in himself, and this culminates in the Antichrist who sets himself up as God.

An illustration from the economic life of this country of ours is illuminating in this connection.

About twenty years ago an amendment to the Constitution of the United States was passed, giving the federal government power to levy taxes on incomes. A great struggle had been waged for and against this for years and years; but finally the amendment passed because, as has been reported, it was agreed that the tax should be a very small per cent of the income. Nevertheless the principle became established. Since then the matter of income tax has been one of degrees. At first only one per cent, then two, and gradually more and more until at present (1936) on some incomes, it is sixty-three per cent. Even higher rates have been suggested and will undoubtedly come. The all important step in bringing about an income tax which can take almost all that a man earns over a given amount was the establishment of the principle under which the first extremely low rate was assessed.

A more specific presentation will be helpful. Modernism denies the miraculous in the Bible. It tries to explain all miracles on a natural basis. After this has been done, it is said that this does not take away from the value of the Bible but improves it, because it is easier to understand. In short, the Bible is lowered to the human, finite plane. The greatest miracle of all recorded in the Bible is the salvation of man— taken from the position of disobedience and rebellion against God and raised not to his original state, but far higher, into the very image of the Son of God and made to be the fullness of Him. To introduce a human element as necessary in this miracle and thereby limit the supernatural in the greatest of miracles, is to limit the supernatural in all that is miraculous. It is but the beginning of Modernism which denies all that is miraculous.

Modernism accepts part of the Bible as truth, but rejects whatever its human reasoning can not explain. The stories of Genesis are nothing but myths, and legend and figurative language. The great prophecies of Daniel and others are said to be history, written after the events had taken place. The truths of the Bible are changed to conform to the imaginations of human minds. Human reason is more important than divine revelation. But is not this the same principle employed in the Arminian arguments? Jesus said "My sheep hear My voice and follow Me." The Arminian argument says: "My sheep hear My voice and *if they* follow Me." Jesus said: "He that believeth . . . hath eternal life." They say: "He that continues to believe receives eternal life as long as he continues to believe." Here also it is a matter of human reason opposed to God's clear revelation.

Modernism by questioning God's Word undermines the foundation of man's faith in God. It causes men to doubt. Anyone who knows anything about university life knows of young men or women who have come back with their spiritual foundation seriously shaken if not gone. Arminianism causes Christian young people especially, but elders too, to doubt the promises of God. They too have their foundations sadly disturbed and their doubts have a blighting effect upon their lives.

Modernism teaches a social gospel. Follow the teachings of Jesus and do good. Live up to the golden rule. That is all that is necessary. It is purely a salvation by good works. Such teaching can never result from a strict adherence to the position that nothing whatsoever in man can contribute to his salvation as held by those who accept eternal security. On the other hand it is but the natural result of the Arminian teachings that unless man does this or does not do that, he will be lost. The principle in Arminianism and Modernism is exactly the same. They differ only in degrees.

There is another similarity in these two, closely related to that of salvation by works. Modernism says: "What is needed is practical Christianity and not doctrinal teaching." Sad to say it is not uncommon to hear the voice of Arminianism complain: "What we need is greater emphasis on practical Christianity rather than doctrinal teaching." Furthermore, it can hardly be denied that relatively little clear doctrinal teaching comes from preachers who are doctrinally Arminian. This is only natural, for the denial of eternal security contradicts in greater or less measure every doctrine of grace. The clearest doctrinal teaching heard these days comes from the lips of those who hold and cherish the truth of the eternal security of the believer.

Thus again, Arminianism by confusing the meaning of the doctrines of grace and by neglecting the teaching of them has but started a tendency which Modernism finishes by rejecting entirely.

THE VALUE OF THE DEATH OF CHRIST

The focal point of this whole discussion is the value of the death of Christ. The doctrine of eternal security rests solidly upon the absolute and unlimited value of the shed blood of Jesus Christ. It is sufficient as a propitiation for every sin committed during the entire life of the believer. Because of the infiniteness of this propitiatory work, the believer has been eternally redeemed from the condemnation of the law and cannot be lost.

Arminianism limits the efficacy of the blood. If a single "must" or "must not" is necessary to become saved or to remain saved, then the shed blood does not have infinite value for salvation of the one who believes. Thus the principle of a limited value of the blood is established, and as this principle is in the realm of the relative, the value given to the blood can be diminished until it reaches the vanishing point; as it does in Modernism, where it is taught that the blood of Jesus was of as great value in His veins as when it was shed on the cross. But there was no propitiation in His blood until it was shed.

Arminianism limits the substitutionary death and thereby says that Christ died as a means of our salvation. "A means" signifies that there are also other means. This is in perfect accord with the teaching that one can be lost because of some human element.

The Modernist will also subscribe to the statement that the death of Christ is a means of salvation. To him it means that Christ in dying gave an example of supreme sacrifice for man to follow. To the Arminian "a means of salvation" means much more than that, but just how much it means one can hardly know. It all depends upon what conditions are added to maintain one's salvation, be it the observance of the Sabbath and the Old Testament tithe, et cetera, or be it the matter of "holding out unto the end." Both Modernists and Arminians can use this same term, because it ascribes only a relative value to the death of Christ.

How different is the value given to the death of Christ upon which eternal security rests! That value is infinite, for it is taught that the shed blood of Christ is the *only* redemption price. It is the only means of being saved from the penalty of sin. That position can never be confused with Modernism, nor can it lead to it.

These are very grave charges. It would have been more agreeable, had this chapter been left unwritten. But the Arminian denial of eternal security is a subtle error that is boring into the very foundation upon which the church is being built, and it is needful that this be known.

33

An Appeal

THE CONSIDERATION of the theme ". . . shall never perish" would be incomplete without an earnest appeal for greater and clearer teaching and preaching of those facts and promises of God which produce assurance in the heart of the believer, and righteousness, godliness and steadfastness in the outward life.

A crying need of the church today is the simple teaching of the doctrines of the grace of God. This is needful both in order to reach the unsaved and that those who are saved might grow in the grace and knowledge of their Lord and Saviour.

When the representative of a firm offers the product of that firm for sale, he is very careful, if he is properly qualified, to show the prospective buyer all of the benefits that will accrue to him if he buys, and what will be lost if the goods are not purchased. He will explain all of the fine qualities of his merchandise and will not neglect to inform the buyer as to the dependability of his own firm to stand back of every article sold.

Is this what is done when salvation is offered? In most cases, No. One often wonders whether or not the unsaved know what it is all about.

Salvation is the greatest thing that any mortal has

204

ever been privileged to offer to another mortal, and
yet what salvation is is seldom explained. That
which is being offered is a deliverance from the
power of Satan; redemption from condemnation of
the law (the penalty for all of one's sins); justification, or a perfectly righteous standing in God's reckoning; a new eternal spiritual life; a citizenship in
heaven; the Holy Spirit as an ever indwelling Power
in the life; the promise of eternal glory in the likeness of God's own Son; and, in addition, the absolute
guarantee that God is fully responsible. What a
proposition God's children and His ministers have
to offer!

And in making a sale it is important that the consideration and terms be clearly explained, for these
are a part of the sale. The consideration is "without
money, and without price." It is all a gift of God in
His own absolute meaning of that word. And the
terms? They are an unconditional acknowledgment
of one's own sinfulness and worthlessness and hopelessly lost condition. "Nothing in my hands I bring.
Simply to Thy cross I cling."

One often wonders: what would be the result in
evangelistic meetings of a consistent setting forth of
these things, to the exclusion of all human emotional
appeal and strategy? If the seller is sold on the proposition which he offers there must be results.

Is the lack of this what Jesus meant when He
said: "The children of this world are in their generation wiser than the children of light." (Luke 16:8)?

And the good salesman, after he has made a sale,

keeps his customer "sold" on the house and the merchandise.

Is not this also needed in the church? Do not those who have been saved need to be taught more and more the meaning of God's wondrous work in salvation, His power and faithfulness for the present, and His promises for the future? Only so will the saved person remain an enthusiastic "customer" of God.

The more a saved person is "sold" on the wonders of salvation and God's faithfulness, the more fervently will he sing with the psalmist, "Truly my soul waiteth upon God; from Him cometh my salvation. He only is my Rock and my Salvation; He is my Defence; I shall not be greatly moved" (Psa. 62:1, 2).

How much need there is for awakening from the lethargy of the present age! Here also the power to revive consists in what God has done, is doing and shall do, as revealed in the doctrines of the grace of God. To urge more practical Christian living without offering as a condition thereof, the doctrines of the grace of God, is to follow Satan's methods of reversing the order of God's plan. God says, "I beseech you . . . by the mercies of God that ye present your bodies." Is that the method that is being used to revive spirtual life in churches? Are the mercies of God (the same doctrines of grace that bring salvation) clearly taught as a basis for the appeal? If not, why not? It is God's plan.

A few years ago, three men were emerging from

a church where they had listened to a simple and effective exposition of Ephesians 2:14-18, by an internationally known Bible teacher. At the door, one man said: "I agree with every word that was said; but our people would not be satisfied with such a simple message."

It was the simplicity of the message that made it effective. If it was well for that great Bible teacher to present his message in simple terms, why is it not good practice for all preachers and teachers to do so? It is the teaching of God's Word in the simplest way possible that many are longing for these days. It is God's Word (not man's preaching) of which He says: "It shall not return unto Me void, but it shall accomplish that which I please, and it shall prosper in the thing whereto I sent it" (Isa. 55:11).